More Praise for *It's All About Who*

"*It's All About Who* tells us exactly how to change the world—how to lead, how to execute, and how to do it all with integrity—from a remarkable man who has spent the last seven decades building a life of extraordinary meaning and exceptional business success. For those starting out on their careers, the book will show how to adopt the leadership fundamentals that matter most. For corporate veterans, it will reignite their passion, commitment to high performance, and belief in what is possible—for leaders and for entire organizations. Leaders at every level should read this essential book. Mandel shows us that each of us is capable of achieving far more than we can ever imagine, if we are just shown the way. This book lights that path brightly."

—**Frederick M. Lawrence**, president, Brandeis University

"Mort Mandel has led an extraordinary life of impact and meaning, and his book is an inspiration to read. It immediately sparks ideas about what you might do differently to be a more effective leader—and a more effective contributor to the world."

—**Jeff Bradach**, cofounder and managing partner, Bridgespan Group

"This book makes it clear that Mort Mandel's success was a function of thoughtful principles and intense personal discipline. Very few can emulate his accomplishments, but everyone can benefit from the wisdom of his well-articulated management philosophy."

—**Stephen Hardis**, former chairman and CEO, Eaton Corp.

"Mort Mandel is an exceptional social innovator and entrepreneur who has created and led highly successful organizations in the independent and business sectors. Mort's insights are spot-on and a must-read for those who aspire to excellence and high achievement in building organizations, developing and leading people, and making a difference in the world."

—**Scott Cowan**, president, Tulane University

"Morton Mandel endows life with multifaceted meanings: physical, social, institutional, academic, intellectual, and cultural. This book is a true opportunity to learn through Morton's own missions how to examine the 'who' of any individual wishing to educate and lead by the five criteria that constitute the right combination of life's meanings: intellectual firepower, values, passion, work ethic, and experience."

—**Menahem Ben-Sasson**, president, Hebrew University of Jerusalem

"This book is a total gem! *It's All About Who* is one of the rare books for leaders across all generations who truly care about achieving unprecedented results. Through real stories that illuminate and inspire, Mort's truth will resonate with both your intellect and your heart—and it's filled with practical ideas about people and priorities you can use immediately. Thank you, Morton Mandel, for taking your precious time to inspire and guide us."

—**Saj-nicole Joni**, confidential CEO advisor; best-selling
author of *The Right Fight*

"In today's changing world, inspiring leaders such as Morton Mandel stand out. Rarely do you find someone whose work in both the for-profit and non-profit worlds has shown that people, execution, and integrity make all the difference. Thanks to *It's All About Who*, we are reminded that leadership is about driving change, making a difference, and having a lasting impact—a single individual has the power to change the world. I highly encourage you to learn from this book how to put his leadership wisdom to work in your life."

—**Rivka Carmi**, president, Ben-Gurion University; pediatrician;
award-winning geneticist

"Mort Mandel is an inspirational leader whose disciplined adherence to his principles and values has produced amazing results in business and philanthropy. The insights he shares in this remarkable book will be valuable to leaders of organizations around the world."

—**Barbara R. Snyder**, president, Case Western Reserve University

"Self-made leader and social entrepreneur Morton Mandel is likely the most successful person you have never heard of . . . until now. In the short time you'll spend reading *It's All About Who*, you'll get every hard-won lesson learned by one of the few CEOs Peter Drucker deemed a master: the ABCs of people, how to solve your most persistent business problems, the rules for a successful partnership, and more. No matter where you are on your leadership path, this book will make an enormous difference in your outcomes. Get your copy today."

—**Laurence Weinzimmer**, Fortune 50 strategist and author of *The Wisdom of
Failure: How to Learn the Tough Leadership Lessons Without Paying the Price*

It's All About Who You Hire, How They Lead,...

and Other *Essential Advice* from a
SELF-MADE LEADER

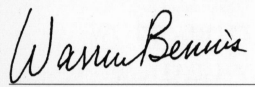

A WARREN BENNIS BOOK

This collection of books is devoted exclusively to new and exemplary contributions to management thought and practice. The books in this series are addressed to thoughtful leaders, executives, and managers of all organizations who are struggling with and committed to responsible change. My hope and goal is to spark new intellectual capital by sharing ideas positioned at an angle to conventional thought—in short, to publish books that disturb the present in the service of a better future.

Books in the Warren Bennis Signature Series

It's All About Who You Hire, How They Lead,...

and Other *Essential Advice* from a SELF-MADE LEADER

Morton L. Mandel

with John A. Byrne

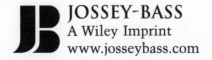

JOSSEY-BASS
A Wiley Imprint
www.josseybass.com

Published by Jossey-Bass
A Wiley Imprint
One Montgomery Street, Suite 1200, San Francisco, CA 94104-4594—www.josseybass.com

Jossey-Bass books and products are available through most bookstores. To contact Jossey-Bass
directly call our Customer Care Department within the U.S. at 800-956-7739, outside the U.S.
at 317-572-3986, or fax 317-572-4002.

Wiley publishes in a variety of print and electronic formats and by print-on-demand. Some
material included with standard print versions of this book may not be included in e-books or in
print-on-demand. If this book refers to media such as a CD or DVD that is not included in the
version you purchased, you may download this material at **http://booksupport.wiley.com**. For
more information about Wiley products, visit **www.wiley.com**.

Library of Congress Cataloging-in-Publication Data
Mandel, Morton L.
  It's all about who you hire, how they lead – and other essential advice from a self-made
leader / Morton L. Mandel, with John A. Byrne. – 1st ed.
    p. cm.
  Includes index.
  ISBN 978-1-118-37988-2 (cloth); ISBN 978-1-118-46139-6 (ebk.);
ISBN 978-1-118-46140-2 (ebk.); ISBN 978-1-118-46141-9 (ebk.)
  1. Leadership. 2. Management. 3. Success in business. I. Byrne, John A. II. Title.
  HD57.7.M354 2013
  658.4'092–dc23

                    2012030060

Printed in the United States of America
FIRST EDITION
HB Printing 10 9 8 7 6 5 4 3 2 1

*This book is dedicated to the loving memory of
my parents, Simon and Rose Mandel; my exceptional wife and life
partner, Barbara; my wonderful, loving children, Amy, Thom, and
Stacy; my brothers, Jack and Joe, my two best friends and lifelong
partners in business and philanthropy; and to all those others who
helped make my dreams come true.*

CONTENTS

EDITOR'S NOTE

Warren Bennis

WE KNOW THAT LEADING PEOPLE AND ORGANIZATIONS IS A NEVER ENDING, often herculean task. It is why there are so many books and articles on the subject; we need this fuel of new ideas, tried-and-true practices, and inspirational real-life stories to help us become better at it. It never gets easier.

Mort Mandel's ideas and experience are exactly the kind of "fuel" anyone, new leader to sage veteran, can learn from. If the primary task of a leader is reminding people of what's important, which I think it is, Mandel's insights are invaluable. For nearly fifty years he, along with his brothers, did just this. They built a company as well as nonprofit organizations that systematically embodied certain standards, like hire with an "enthusiastic yes" or not at all, insist on transparency . . . or pay a big price, be scrupulously honest, and many more you will find here. On every page here, Mort is telling you "Listen to me. I know. I have been around the block a few times and have learned a few things. Here is a playbook."

Having studied and written about leadership now for many years, I have to say that the folks who still truly inspire me are the ones who have *done it* successfully. There are few in this category, and of them Mort Mandel stands out. People often ask me for leadership advice. I point them to the true masters. That would be Mort, who has walked the talk, and the results speak for themselves.

FOREWORD

John A. Byrne

OVER THE COURSE OF A LONG CAREER IN JOURNALISM, I've met and interviewed many of this generation's greatest corporate leaders: Jack Welch, Andy Grove, John Chambers, A. G. Lafley, and Jeff Immelt, among countless others. Then, one day out of the blue, I received a telephone call from a friend who asked me whether I had ever heard of Mort Mandel. I had to confess, I hadn't. But the phone call led to a meeting and then to numerous interviews and the book in your hands.

Management sage Peter Drucker once put Mort in the company of Andy Grove and Jack Welch. I think he did Mort an injustice. Unlike a Jack Welch, an Andy Grove, or a Lee Iacocca, whose corporate achievements define their public personas, Mort has lived in two worlds all of his years: the world of profit and the world of social impact. Even as the chairman and CEO of a New York Stock Exchange company for more than three decades, he was spending as much as a third of his time in the social sector. Mort strongly believes that his experience in the social sector made him a better corporate executive, just as he is convinced that what he learned in business made him a more effective social capitalist.

What makes Mort unusual, if not unique, is his selflessness in pursuing a life of purpose. From his earliest days, he understood that there was much more to a successful life than building wealth—though as a self-made billionaire, his is a quintessential rags-to-riches story. Mort understood that a life without meaning, purpose, and commitment isn't a life at all. So he devoted a large share of his time, while building his business with his brothers, to improving the human condition by bringing better leadership to social causes.

As a writer helping Mort tell his remarkable story, I could easily have lapsed into a modern-day version of Horatio Alger. After a childhood spent in the most humble of circumstances, Mort and his two older brothers scraped together $900 in 1940 and went into business as a distributor of auto parts. From a Cleveland storefront on Euclid Avenue, the brothers built Premier Industrial Corp. into a national company that by 1960 went public and in 1964 was listed on the New York Stock Exchange. For thirty-four out of Premier's thirty-six years, Mort led Premier as CEO to record earnings, selling what many would consider fairly humdrum products—nuts and bolts, circuit breakers, chemicals, lubricating oil, and firefighting equipment.

A hundred dollars invested in Premier stock in 1960, when Mort led the company's public offering, had grown in value to $23,200 by 1996, when Premier merged with England-based Farnell Electronics in a $3 billion deal. That comes out to a 232-times return, even without accounting for the reinvestment of some $417 million in dividends the company paid to shareholders during that period.

What's more, this record was accomplished the old-fashioned way—with hard work and uncommon integrity. There was no high finance, balance sheet tricks, junk bonds, tax dodges, or other financial gimmickry. Throughout its history, Premier boasted an immaculate balance sheet and a clean income statement, with virtually no debt, generous cash flow, and consistently high returns on capital. The financial results are testimony to exceptionally high standards and careful control of risk.

Since the sale of Premier, Mort and his brothers have built a highly successful private trust company, Parkwood Corp., to manage their wealth; created a private equity firm in Israel that owns and runs two fascinating businesses; and have devoted much of their time to philanthropic efforts that, among other things, have nurtured a new generation of social leaders in Israel and have lent sorely needed support for the humanities in both the United States and Israel. That latter commitment—backed by a recent investment of some $50 million in funding—comes from Mort's strongly held belief that a civil and engaged society must learn the wisdom of its forefathers, the philosophers, historians, and writers from whose knowledge and experience all of us can benefit.

Telling Mort's story—and sharing with readers the powerful ideas that led to this success—would ordinarily be enough. But it wouldn't do Mort's journey or his beliefs justice. As a result, *It's All About Who You Hire, How They Lead, . . . and Other* Essential Advice *from a Self-Made Leader* is not your typical CEO biography, nor is it yet another management book to add to a wonderful bookshelf loaded with advice and counsel from such wise thinkers as Peter Drucker, Tom Peters, and Jim Collins. Instead, it is the story of a man and the ideas that have allowed him to be enormously successful in business and also to craft a life of significance.

For all of Mort's corporate accomplishments, his greatest source of pride is in the social sector. One example is the recruiting and training of a corps of 450 outstanding leaders who are transforming K–12 education in Israel, building schools in which Arabs and

Israelis sit side by side as classmates, and also bringing together religious and secular students in the same schools. No less crucial, Mort has helped shape the lives of a multitude of Jews by devoting extraordinary time and money to strengthen the leadership and effectiveness of Jewish Community Centers in America and also around the world. Among other kudos, Mort received an award from President Ronald Reagan at a ceremony in the Rose Garden at the White House for his leadership in neighborhood renewal and revitalization in Cleveland. For his considerable contributions to the humanities, Mort was recently elected to membership in the American Academy of Arts and Sciences in the company of a number of others, including Ford Motor CEO Alan Mulally, jazz icon Dave Brubeck, documentary filmmaker Ken Burns, and songwriter Paul Simon.

What Mort learned about management and leadership as a hands-on volunteer leader and philanthropist has been as profound as what he learned building a highly successful growth company. He believes that running the United Way or IBM is much the same, except in the measurement of outcomes. IBM generates profit; United Way touches and improves lives. What they share in common to get those results is great leadership, disciplined execution, and a rich culture built on respect, fairness, decency, and integrity.

Mort strongly believes that one of the largest problems hampering the impact of nonprofits is that social sector leaders fail to devote enough time and thought to the management issues that will build the kind of institution that will ultimately be most helpful to the people they are trying to serve.

Respect for the individual, superior client service, and the pursuit of excellence are core values that can deliver as much impact in the social world as in the corporate world. These ideas work in all settings. These guiding principles apply to all firms that serve people, whether they are universities, hospitals, charitable organizations, or multinational corporations. They are the essence of great leadership—and the basis of Mort's belief that a single individual has the power to change the world.

(My favorite story about Mort involves the only time one of his businesses suffered a work stoppage. Over a four-day period, in the dead of a winter in the mid-1990s, strikers picketed outside his plant in Wooster, Ohio. Mort saw to it that the company took a pickup truck, filled it with sandwiches and Thermos bottles full of hot coffee and tea, and made sure that the employees striking against him were well fed on the picket line. Mort considered those employees members of his extended family. Some of them had worked for Premier for twenty-five years. Sons followed fathers in that plant. "Why wouldn't we treat them well?" asks Mort. Why, indeed.)

With his mind, his heart, his hands, and his money, Mort Mandel has created a life of meaning. As a result, he has much to teach all of us—MBA candidates, entrepreneurs, and managers and executives of companies, hospitals, schools, and nonprofit enterprises. What does it take to start and build an enduring institution from the ground up? What does it take to transform a social enterprise into a high-performing organization that touches the lives of people around the world? What does it take to live a life of which you can be proud? The answers to these questions can be found in the lessons Mort teaches us.

Most remarkable, perhaps, is that even at the age of ninety, Mort does not merely welcome the future but believes that he still has a firm hand in shaping that future and lighting a few more candles in an often dark world sorely in need of light.

You'll be better for knowing him.

PROLOGUE

IN ONE OF THE EARLIEST PHOTOGRAPHS OF MYSELF, I'm not much more than three years old. Wearing a long-sleeve white shirt and overalls, I'm sitting on the step in the back of my parents' dry goods store in Cleveland, Ohio, that led to our small apartment. My eyes are fixed with a mixture of awe and admiration on the woman across the room.

The woman is my mother, the single greatest influence on my life. Almost everything I am, almost everything I became, I owe to her—from the core values that formed the foundation of my life—integrity, respect, honesty, and generosity—to the highly effective habits of a life of discipline, reason, entrepreneurship, and hard work. Ma gave me the moral compass that helped instill purpose in my life and the lives of my sister, Meriam, and my two older brothers, Jack and Joe. So it's fascinating to me that my three-year-old eyes are drawn by the quality of her strength and her presence.

In a black-and-white picture taken in 1924, my mother is standing behind the wooden counter of her store, confident and strong, remarkably and some might say surprisingly proud, given the circumstances captured in the photo. There are no customers in the place. The inventory is sparse. There's more space between the dresses on the back racks than there are dresses. By today's standards, it's old, poorly lit, and not very inviting.

The picture shows a struggling business that is barely surviving. Yet my mother betrays no sign of disappointment. If anything, she is full of pride and self-assurance. With dark, penetrating eyes, she stares at the lens of the camera being held by Meriam. She seems oblivious to the plain environment around her. In fact, she looks proud enough to have owned a successful business, not one inadequately stocked with whatever she could convince the wholesalers to sell her.

That photograph says a lot about my mother and ultimately about me. My mother was not merely a survivor. She was a warrior. She literally carried my sister and two brothers through two of the great tragedies of her time: a World War that engulfed her homeland, and terrifying anti-Jewish pogroms that led to the beatings and deaths of scores of innocent Jews in Poland. My father had already left for America in 1913, planning to send for his family once he became settled in Ohio. A year after he arrived, however, World War I erupted, and my mother and siblings were temporarily lost to him, as they struggled to evade the horrors and dangers of war.

On her own at the age of twenty-six, Ma willed herself through a war-torn Poland filled with burdens and hardships. To keep her children alive, she occasionally smuggled food across war lines. Once, a Cossack stabbed her with his sword, leaving a permanent scar on one of her thighs. She hid her children in a nearby school to save them from violent beatings, if not death. At other times, she concealed my brothers and sister in the haystacks of a nearby cornfield or in the attic of a sympathetic Polish neighbor who was willing to risk her life to save them from harm.

In those years, Galicia in southern Poland was a forbidding place for its large Jewish population. Anti-Semitism was rampant. My late brother Jack recalled going into the bathroom of a church at the age of five. While he was standing at a urinal, someone tapped him on the shoulder, and when he saw that Jack had been circumcised, he shouted "Yid, get out of here!" Food was scarce. Jack remembers longing for meat so badly that he once suggested to my mother that a cat be killed for food. "You can't do that," he recalls my mother telling him. "Cats aren't kosher."

Much worse than a racist comment or an empty stomach, though, were the pogroms, the riots meant to wreak havoc and fear on the Jewish neighborhoods. Occasionally on Friday nights, angry, drunken mobs roamed the unpaved streets. The homes of Jews were routinely invaded and looted; people were clubbed and trampled to death. My mother and siblings were eyewitnesses to unspeakable atrocities and brutalities.

After waking one morning to streets strewn with body parts and blood, the result of an especially horrifying pogrom, my mother became determined to get herself and her children to America. With the help of the Red Cross, my mother safely got her children to Rotterdam and onto a ship, the *New Amsterdam*, that crossed the Atlantic and reunited the family with my father. It's why my brother Jack often called my mother "a woman of valor." It's why my brother Joe says that no matter what the dangers, my mother would have figured out a way to save them.

When she and her children made the passage from Europe to America, my brothers were so used to being hungry that they gathered an oversupply of herring and bread on the boat and hid the extra food in the pillowcases of their bunk beds in steerage. It was the first time in their lives they saw more food than they could eat. When they finally arrived at Ellis Island in June of 1920, my mother had all of $1.50 in her pocket. They were so forlorn and scraggly looking that my brother Jack joked that he was surprised our father didn't disavow his family on sight and run away. My brothers and sister spoke only Yiddish. Rose, my mother, was just thirty-three years old. Meriam was ten; Jack was eight, and Joe was six. This was the first time our father laid eyes on Joe. I would come into this American world fifteen months later on September 19, 1921.

As it turned out, the dry goods store in the picture would fail, and this was the second store my parents owned that would go under. We moved from one apartment on the east side of Cleveland to another because my parents often couldn't come up with the monthly rent. I slept in a room I shared with my two brothers, and I wore hand-me-downs. Yet we never thought of ourselves as poor. No doubt, this is because of the love and devotion my parents showed each other and us. If anything, I felt powerfully fulfilled because of the honesty, decency, generosity, and kindness my parents showed and taught us. I soaked up those values and beliefs through osmosis, and they have become the guideposts for my life.

When my father developed multiple sclerosis in his mid-thirties and eventually became completely bedridden, my mother served as his caregiver and sold clothing out of suitcases on city streets to put food on the table. It was my mother's perseverance, her tenacity, her utter devotion to her children that not only kept us alive and well but ultimately helped make us enormously successful.

My bond with her was profound. She would come home from work during my school years to serve me lunch, often a scoop of baked beans and a roll, and then take the streetcar downtown to buy more things from a wholesaler to sell door-to-door in the morning. When I enlisted in the U.S. Army during World War II,

I wrote her every day I was in uniform, and she wrote back every day as well. I was probably the only soldier at mail call who was never disappointed.

Truth is, she made the American dream our dream. From this poor, humble background, my brothers and I created a business that would eventually make all three of us billionaires and fifty-six of our six thousand employees millionaires. We started out seeking to earn a living, to become financially comfortable, and ended up with financial success far beyond our wildest expectations.

From a tiny company that sold auto parts in the 1940s, we built a global distributor of industrial and electronic parts with sixteen divisions and nearly a billion dollars in annual revenue. That company, Premier Industrial Corp., was a profit-making machine. We had succeeded in converting what could have been a commodity business into a true value-added business with strong margins. My brothers and I stopped thinking about money. We simply thought about winning and giving back.

Through all these thirty-six years, we often reflected on what our mother taught us—both consciously and subconsciously—and I attribute a lot of our success to the values and behaviors we absorbed from her. We ran a business that was principled, not opportunistic, always trying to do what was best for our employees and our customers. While most businesses focused heavily on the what and the how, we put our emphasis on the who—finding the best and most passionate people, getting them in the right jobs, and motivating them to higher levels of excellence. We placed special emphasis on two core objectives: first-class leadership and disciplined execution. Early on, we learned that if you found a customer need and filled it, success would inevitably follow.

For me, business became an art form. If I were an architect, I'd want to build a cathedral or an art museum—not put up garages or warehouses. Creating a world-class business institution was such a challenge. We adhered to our core business principles, which have stood the test of time: "Killing Yourself for Your Customer," "Always Trying to Raise the Bar," and "A Focus on Our People." Those simple aphorisms have a profound effect on a business when you live by them. That's exactly what we did. Those ideas allowed us to take a business in which we invested $900 in 1940 and transform it into a public corporation that we merged for $3 billion some fifty-six years later.

We were lucky, too, to realize early in our lives that when true wealth became a by-product of our success, we did not own that wealth, but rather were merely its custodian, charged with using it for worthy purposes. Even though our family had little, my mother often gave what she could to others, whether a sandwich to a hungry man who showed up at our door or a few dollars to a neighbor who needed to buy a dress for her child. Ma had a pushke, a tin can, into which spare change was dropped for helping others. It was a permanent fixture in our apartments, a center of caring and kindness, even though we had so little at the time. We were taught the joy and obligation of helping others. This has made our lives more meaningful, and had an everlasting impact on my brothers and me.

It's why my brothers and I used our business success to also become social entrepreneurs at an early age, long before we acquired true wealth. The world can be a dark and chaotic place. My life's goal is to light as many candles as possible to brighten the prospects of the less fortunate in this world. Yes, I've been lucky to make more money than I could ever need in my lifetime, but even more important, I've been very fortunate to discover that by giving back, I could find an extraordinary amount of meaning along the way.

I've served as chief volunteer officer for a large number of high-impact community organizations that tried to provide light in many places of darkness. I have founded, either alone or with others, more than a dozen 501(c)(3) nonprofit organizations aimed at improving the quality of professional leadership in the social sector, rehabilitating inner cities, and revitalizing Jewish education around the world. I didn't do this as a well-intentioned person who lends his name to a cause; instead, I rolled up my sleeves and applied every ounce of my ability to lead and manage organizations in the social sector, trying to ensure that our efforts reached as many people as possible. Those experiences touched my life in serious ways: I owe much of my sense of self-worth to my deep commitment and immersion in the nonprofit sector.

I write this book because I believe that my story and my ideas, though perhaps not unique, are both enduring and of possible value to others. I know there are some who believe the American Dream has become more elusive. I don't. There is as much opportunity for smart, creative, hard-working entrepreneurs today as there was back in 1940 when my brothers and I went into business together. If I could live my full life again, turn back the clock to that day in 1940 when I had only a few dollars to my name, I would do the same thing in a heartbeat. One thing is for sure: I owe much of my success to the strong woman in that dry goods store so many years ago.

CHAPTER 1

It's All About Who

IF YOU ASKED ME TO SUM UP EVERYTHING I KNOW IN THE FEWEST WORDS, I would do it in just four: "It's all about who."

All my adult life—from the businesses we started to the businesses we bought, from the charitable causes we've created to those we serve— I've been completely devoted to hiring and keeping extraordinary people. This isn't just talk or wishful thinking. My belief in the power of exceptional leadership is the most important principle I follow.

If you studied the CEOs of the largest Fortune 500 companies, I'd bet that less than 10 percent of them would be on fire about this the way I am. Jack Welch and Bill Gates know this and are prime standard-setters. When Welch was CEO of General Electric, he said, "I don't want GE to be known as the best product factory. I want it to be known as the best people factory." Every world-class organization is indeed a people factory because everything depends on people. All the rest is commentary.

It's why I also strongly believe in the ability of a single extraordinary person to change the world.

The forces that influence an institution the most are the human forces—the people who manage it, inspire it, lead it, and build it.

And success starts at the top. If you look at the history of the world, it's largely the history of exceptional people, for good or for bad—Abraham Lincoln and Winston Churchill, for good; Josef Stalin, for bad. Leadership is what makes an organization soar, or fly a flat line to mediocrity, or, sadly, plummet to the ground. The great institutions of the world—whether they are for-profit or nonprofit enterprises—are defined by the quality of their leadership and the people who follow those leaders.

When you have the right people in the right seats on the right bus, as Jim Collins puts it, something magical happens. Smart strategy, strong culture, and perfect execution tend to follow. When you have mediocre people leading your team, it negatively impacts strategy and culture, and perfect execution tends to be very unlikely.

Most people instinctively know this to be true. But many leaders do not make the commitment needed to build a team with only the best people. More often, organizations compromise. A company has open positions it needs to fill. They have three people to promote. They're under pressure from colleagues or customers to fill each job because work needs to get done. So they make the compromised choice. They interview a handful of outside applicants and say yes quickly to fill a position, or they promote someone from within who they're only mildly positive about. There is compromise everywhere. That's why there are so many B and even C players in so many important positions.

Sometimes, employers are not willing to pay up for the best talent. They seek to pay less than what's needed to acquire excellence. That is a poor trade when they could seek a highly qualified employee whose contribution to the organization can be worth many times the cost. Exceptional people are likely to produce more

2

growth and more benefit than people who are average and will work for less.

I don't settle. I will spend weeks, months, even years recruiting, sifting through available people to find the extraordinary. The dream of every leader should be to have the right person in the right job at the right time. It's a very challenging goal. Hiring and promoting are both highly subjective. Although we may never achieve perfection, that's what we should want.

Only recently, I waited four years to hire the person I wanted to succeed me as head of the Mandel Foundation. I had gotten to know Jehuda Reinharz, then president of Brandeis University, over the years. So had my wife, Barbara, who sits on the board of trustees at Brandeis. Jehuda had joined the Mandel Foundation board in 2005. In my book, he is a world-class educator, a widely respected scholar, a humanitarian, and an undisputed A player. So I pursued him for years before getting him to accept the job. I'll let Jehuda tell the story:

> Mort's way of doing things is gradual. Four years ago, he began to broach this idea. I was visiting him in Palm Beach, and we went for a walk along the beach. He asked me what I planned to do after I left the presidency at Brandeis. I had been president for twelve years, and I had two years to go on my third five-year term.
>
> "Let's talk about what you're going to do," Mort said. "Would you be interested in working with us?"
>
> "Yes," I told him. "What do you have in mind?"
>
> Over time, we started talking about more specific things. He asked me where would I want to live, how would I work with him, how much should I be paid. Two years prior to the end of my last term, we put together a list of the things we agreed to: how often I would see him, how we would communicate. It was very detailed.
>
> I felt it was my duty to tell the board at Brandeis that this would be my last term. When I did, they started working on my wife, Shula, and me

and ultimately made a very sweet deal for me to stay a fourth term. I had to tell Mort immediately, of course, and I knew it was going to be a difficult discussion. I didn't want it to impact our friendship. There was no way I was going to do it on the phone. It was hard for me to disappoint him.

So I went to New York in the fall of 2008 to see him at his apartment. He did not get angry. He listened carefully. And then he said, "Tell me why."

I told him I wanted to finish some of the projects I started, and I wanted to make sure that all of the initiatives and programs already in place were in good shape. The conversation was very difficult for me, but Mort put me at ease. He didn't torture me. Before I left his apartment, he said to me, "I might try to find someone else." I left, started my fourth term at Brandeis, and it was as if nothing had happened. Half-jokingly, Mort would sometimes needle me and say, "I still like you."

Then, a year ago, I announced to the board I would leave early, before my last term was up. Mort knew immediately because his wife, Barbara, is on the Brandeis board. He called me and said, "Well, do you want to work with us now?"

My decision was to go with Mort. Frankly, I did so because I believe in what the Mandel Foundation does. He's enormously smart, and I respect him. I'm working for him because I believe in what he does. I felt enormously honored the first time around. He was willing to wait four years before my term was over.

Mort was so gracious. He said, "I have a list of candidates that consists of one person. That person would be a home run for me and for the foundation. It's you." When people knew I was leaving Brandeis, I had six other offers. When my wife asked, "Why Mort?" I told her that when I get up every morning, I want to be able to say that the person I'll be spending my day with is someone I respect and is fun to work with. That was critically important to me. I don't know anyone who works as hard at philanthropy as Mort does. He really believes he has made and will continue to make this a better world. I respect that.

To me, Jehuda was what I call an "enthusiastic yes." He shares the vision and the passion that my brothers and I have for our philanthropic work. In January 2011, Jehuda started as president of the foundation. He is an exceptional leader who will not merely continue the foundation program but will enrich it. That's worth waiting for, and that's worth being enthusiastic about.

I have to rate a candidate as an enthusiastic yes to hire him or her. On occasion, I turn down a candidate recommended to me by my colleagues. I'm sure that my colleagues are sometimes frustrated by some of these decisions, but they trust me and ask, "What did I miss?" They know I'm focused like a laser on getting the absolute best person in the job. Every time I turn down a candidate who made it through a series of interviews, I'm also reminding everyone that hiring the best people in the world is what we're all about.

There's one mistake I made earlier in my business life when it comes to people: only hiring when there was a defined need. One day, I realized that if we could afford it, it's just as important to hire exceptionally talented people even when you don't have an opening. On occasion, when we found a gifted person, an A player beyond doubt, we'd hire her and "park" her in the organization. At first, we would just give the person something to do. Always, after a few months, she was working ten-hour days and making a big contribution. Inevitably, we found an important role for her, or she found it on her own. I never regretted hiring an A player.

What do I look for? Five key things, in this order.

1. Intellectual firepower
2. Values
3. Passion
4. Work ethic
5. Experience

I always put brainpower first because intellect is the most important of the raw materials we work with. From intelligence comes thoughtful analysis, asking the right questions, good judgment, and better decisions. I want the smartest people I can find to join our organization. High-potential people like to be with other high-potential people. When I interview candidates, I'll often ask them to bring me through their lives. I want to know what their family history is. I want to know how well candidates performed in high school and college. I want to know whether they also reached beyond their academic achievements to demonstrate some leadership potential.

Frankly, I want to know if their grade-point average (GPA) was 2.7 or 3.9 out of a possible 4.0. Even if they've been out of school for many years, a GPA can represent four years of evaluation, not a sixty-minute impression during a brief interview on a busy day. It may not be necessarily true that a 3.9 GPA will do better than a 2.7, but the odds are with you. Just like the manager of a baseball team who puts a right-handed pitcher on the mound to face a right-handed batter in a crucial at-bat, I play the odds.

So I'm looking for the Phi Beta Kappa, the captain of the debating team, the president of the student council. It's no coincidence that seventeen presidents of the United States, thirty-seven U.S. Supreme Court justices, and 131 Nobel laureates have been members of Phi Beta Kappa.

I'm also looking for the person who rose quickly in another organization and was rewarded with an important leadership job. What challenges did that executive overcome to get something meaningful done? How did that person apply his intelligence to the job to make something happen?

My hurdle for brainpower is high, but once it's jumped I'm on to the next most important attribute of success: values. Ultimately, all the intelligence in the world isn't going to help a person who lacks basic integrity and compassion for other human beings. I'm looking for honesty, decency, respect, kindness, generosity, and consideration.

Getting a fix on a person's values is admittedly difficult. Values are easier to discern once you have a person on staff, but much harder to recognize in an interview. You have to sense them. I can pick up some fairly good clues by the way candidates speak about their parents, their teachers, their role models in life. I want people who have been inspired by others, who are generous in giving credit to those who made a difference in their lives. I'm looking for people who want to help others in need, who have demonstrated kindness and consideration to the disadvantaged. Some of this may be subtle. It's what you can interpret from a tone of voice or a face lighting up. But this tells me a lot about a person's purpose in life.

Passion has become an overused word in recent years. Still, it's the level of enthusiasm and interest in work and life that makes someone stand out above the rest. It's a fire that burns deeply within us. Once tapped, it can bring you to places that few other people can go.

Unlike values, passion is easy to spot. You either have it or you don't. There is a spirit or fervor in people who have passion. You can often feel their energy. They also are infectious team members. They ignite the passion in others. They get others to care as much as they do about accomplishing the possible and the seemingly impossible.

My fourth hiring attribute is work ethic. I work hard. I do so because I'm passionate about the work I do, and I feel good when I'm highly productive. I expect the same from the people we hire. We want people who embrace work, who understand that it's not something you do only to earn a living, but rather something that can help define who you are in this life.

During interviews, I try to get a feel for people who have a strong work ethic. You get that from learning they worked during high school and college, whether they worked weekends, what they sacrificed at times to work instead of play. At some level, work is about sacrifice: giving up some time with your friends or your family to perform your job at the highest possible level of excellence.

Finally, we come to experience. Experience, though important, is the last of the five things I look for because it's something you can provide your staff. We can't give them more intellect, better values, passion, or a strong work ethic. But we can give them experience by providing an opportunity to learn a discipline or a job. That's why we can make a compromise when it comes to experience, but we will never compromise on the first four.

When I recruit talent, I want to be as sure as possible that the person I'm hiring has all of these attributes. That requires patience and work. And then I will do whatever it takes to bring that exceptional person on board. Only last year, I found someone I came to believe would make an ideal chief investment officer for Parkwood Corp., our trust company based in Cleveland that manages the family's interests. This person would eventually succeed me as the person who would have the final say on our investments. I'll let Jon McCloskey tell the story of how he came aboard.

I had to meet Mort five times during the recruitment process over a five-month period—the first time in New York City at his apartment, then in Palm Beach at his home, then in Cleveland, and in Palm Beach again. They were all-day affairs. I slept overnight in his home twice. Honestly, I wondered what I was going to say for twenty-four hours while with him. At the end, it's the reason I accepted his offer. Mort invests a lot of time in getting it right. He spent the time to get to really know me—no one else ever did.

It was a sign of his true investment in people. All along the way, he was straight and honest. He'd say, "Let the process play out. We'll meet again and I'll let you know if my green light is still on, and you let me know if your green light is on. Once it's red or yellow, we can be big boys and part ways." As it turned out, there never was a yellow or red light.

After four of the five meetings, Mort asked me to come to Cleveland and bring my wife, Alison. I wasn't surprised that it was part of his due diligence. I still didn't have an offer, but clearly Mort was getting ready to give me one. We lived in San Diego, and Mort wanted to make sure my wife would come with her eyes wide open. He didn't want me to come and have my wife not like it and be unhappy. So he was retiring those risks one at a time.

We flew to Cleveland in early January, and when we left San Diego it was seventy-two degrees and sunny. When we reached Cleveland, it was cold and gray, and snow was everywhere. When the plane descended through the clouds, it was like breaking through the atmosphere and going to Mars. I'm thinking to myself, "This is not going well." We rented a car, and I had to scrape the ice off the windshield. The snow was falling so hard I couldn't see the road ahead of me. It was all of ten degrees, and we were in a complete, white-out blizzard.

Mort met us for dinner that evening, and he was super charming. Despite the weather, Alison was sold. She felt so good about the dinner we had with Mort that she impulsively gave him a big hug as we were leaving.

Years ago, the famous management guru Peter Drucker sat down with me and gave me some of the best advice I have ever received. I asked him how we could make our company grow faster. He told me to put my best person on my biggest opportunity.

Skeptical, I asked Peter a tough question: "If my best person is a dentist, would I put him in charge of running a brass foundry?"

Peter didn't hesitate even a moment to answer.

"Yes," he insisted. "Let me tell you what that dentist will do if he's your best person. He'll walk into that building, tour the plant, and speak to the employees. He'll immediately realize he doesn't know anything about a brass foundry. But he's going to get his people together and figure it out. He'll try to find someone on that team who is highly qualified to run the plant. If he doesn't come up with one, he'll find the best foundry man in the country. The dentist will soon learn how to improve the leadership and the culture and reinforce the values. He'll know the importance you attach to perfect execution and killing oneself for the customer."

In my view, what makes institutions great is all the soft stuff, which I think is the hardest stuff in business.

CHAPTER 2

The ABC's of People

IF YOU BELIEVE THAT PEOPLE TRULY MATTER, you have to hire the very best. You have to do what most people find even more difficult: you have to remove people who can't do the job well enough and who resist efforts to improve. The first time I had to switch out a leader from a position of authority was in the social sector, not in the for-profit world. At age thirty-two, in 1953, I had become the president of Cleveland's Jewish Community Center (JCC). I inherited an executive director who was a high-quality person and a fine social worker, but who totally lacked leadership skills.

It's not an uncommon situation. The social sector has many good, well-intentioned people who are not effective institution leaders. They are in leadership roles because they are trained to help people, but often lack the skills needed to effectively lead their institution. This well-meaning man was one of them. One of the symptoms of his inability to lead could be found in the meetings of the board of trustees. These board meetings, scheduled for 8 PM, often wouldn't start until close to 9 PM. Surprisingly, there was little regard for board members' time or schedules, and few of them seemed to care. When I tried to get the executive director to do something about it, he shrugged his shoulders. It was the way he approached many administrative aspects of his job.

After I became president, I was determined to actually start our meetings on time. The executive director was nervous at the thought. At the very first meeting I chaired, 8 PM came, and nobody showed up. I looked up at the clock at 8:15, and still no one was in the room except the director and me. So we shut the door to the conference room, and I began reading aloud the *Wall Street Journal*. In walked one person at 8:20, shocked that the door was closed and that the meeting, at least in principle, had begun. At 8:50, most of the members were finally in the room.

I adjourned the session exactly as scheduled at 10 PM. I told everyone I want to respect our promise to get directors out by that time, so we needed to begin our meetings on time. At the next session, I started the meeting at 8:10, and still almost no one was there. By perhaps the fourth meeting, we started at 8:10, and almost everyone was there.

But, of course, running a meeting effectively, with a well-planned agenda, wasn't the only problem. Many of the board members were not sufficiently engaged. It was an organization that just got by day to day. After six months of trying to improve the executive director's performance, and achieving only limited success, we called the national organization of the JCC movement and said, "We need a better professional leader." The national organization sent us some resumes, and, in due course, our search committee hired a replacement. Before the search began, I sat down with the current executive director and explained what we were going to do, and the considerate way we planned to bring about his separation. He completely understood. The national JCC organization then found him another position for which he was qualified, and he left.

In essence, we sought to replace a C leader with an A leader and believed it would make a world of difference. Fortunately, we found and hired a highly qualified executive director named Herman Eigen. Trained as a social worker, he had very successfully managed the JCC in Buffalo, New York. He was smart, passionate, idealistic, and imaginative. He brought fresh ideas and unlimited energy to the job. We reorganized and upgraded the board and staff. Buoyed by this renewed energy, we raised millions of dollars for a new facility and built a new, up-to-date JCC. Herman stayed on as executive director for fifteen years, until his retirement. He was wonderful!

He changed us from a mom-and-pop store into a first-class JCC. And in the process, I learned a lot from him, most surprisingly that you run a nonprofit the same way you run a for-profit business. I learned forever the importance of recruiting and keeping the very best people, such that the goal to get A's on my team became a cornerstone of my leadership philosophy. Herman may have been the first person to help me understand the miraculous value of an A player.

It's a lesson that is particularly difficult for many leaders, especially in the nonprofit world, which naturally attracts people who want to be helpful to underperforming staff. Steve Hoffman, a long-time board member of our foundation and the president and CEO of the Jewish Federation of Cleveland, explains this well:

> In the past, I was trained as a social worker. So I would be much more focused on how I help a person who is performing below expectations. That is basically the wrong stance. We want to help everybody develop, but if someone can't improve their work ethic or they just don't have it, I have to say we don't owe someone a job.
>
> What I learned from Mort is that a person who is performing well below expectations is hurting the organization. That person pulls

everyone else down. Our first loyalty needs to be to the organization because that is why people are contributing money to us to achieve our objectives.

Now, I always ask Mort's simple question: "Knowing what we know today, would we hire this person again?" If the answer is no, you've almost made a decision. It becomes self-evident to everyone. You are no longer worrying about the person or their family. By not making that decision, who pays the price? The organization pays the price, and your fellow employees pay the price.

People talk about these things but don't do them. Most want to be seen as "nice" people. When that light bulb went off in my head, it made a world of difference.

I'm a realist. Not everyone has what it takes to assume a leadership role. Intelligence is not a given, nor is passion, values, or work ethic. Many people shun leadership responsibility. Only a few possess what it takes to be truly successful leaders. I call such people A's.

Over the course of my career, I've personally interviewed and helped hire many people, from personal assistants to institution presidents. In the early days of Premier, I was, in actual practice, the personnel department. To fill a single opening, we would go through many resumes, interview five to ten candidates, and then, we hoped, hire one. Because we were so thorough, only a very small number were outright failures.

By and large, the few serious mistakes were people who turned out to be C's. Those hires hurt an organization because like the JCC executive director I had to replace, they fill seats that could be occupied by more effective players. Retaining underperforming senior executives keeps the A's out. Never settle for fair when you can have better by raising your standards.

I believe this more strongly today than ever. I have to concede that in my earlier years I was not nearly as sensitive as I am now to what it takes to be excellent. It's different when you not only believe in a principle but also completely internalize it.

My current team knows this well. To sustain our present world-class organization, we insist that everyone aim to hire only A's.

Mark Madeja, vice president and director of investment operations at Parkwood Corp., can tell you a story from the trenches:

> We had one candidate for an internal audit job who was not a slam-dunk person. Four of us interviewed her and then we sent her on to Mort. We all thought she should be hired. She could fill the role and do a fine job in it. And Mort said, "She's a B," and would not approve her. At first, it was difficult. If you have a need, you want to get someone in there, especially if they are good enough. This position was open for eight months. In this case, it meant the work wasn't being done. The longer you go without it, the further you fall behind. So it was frustrating.
>
> I thought she was good enough, and I would have hired her. But Mort will wait for an A. Every time, it's got to be an enthusiastic yes, or it is a no. This candidate had plenty of brainpower. She had enthusiasm. If she fell short, it was on passion and interpersonal skills. It's tough to put my finger on it. There was nothing we could check in the rating box that would have disqualified her. What I learned from that experience is to hold out for the enthusiastic yes.

That is a bedrock principle with me. If my team finds a "qualified" candidate for a job, my question is, "Can you honestly and genuinely tell me you're enthusiastically in favor of hiring this person? You can only give me three answers: an enthusiastic yes, a maybe, or a sure no." If the candidate receives a "weak yes," that answer disqualifies the person because it increases the chance that you'll hire a B or even a C.

What I have discovered is that B's can prevent an organization from achieving much greater accomplishments. The C players generally get fired or quit because they can't meet the standards. But the B players hang on. They bat .270 and don't make many errors in the field, but they can't help you win the pennant. They cheat you from achieving all you could. Even worse, you probably won't know what you've failed to achieve—all because you had a B player with whom you were comfortable, in a job where you could have had an A.

The latest example of the enormous benefits of having an A in a key job is at our Phoenica Glass Works in Yerucham, Israel. We bought Phoenica, which makes glass bottles, in 2005 from a private equity firm based in the United Kingdom. It was losing money; the factory was relatively inefficient; the poor in-plant safety record was a serious concern; and the tension between the union leadership in the plant and the management was so thick you could touch it. In the last three years, we have replaced virtually the entire senior management team—seven of the top eight executives. The rank-and-file workforce of some 250 employees, however, remained the same.

The newly installed leadership team of A players has led to a total transformation of the company, and this has resulted in an almost perfect set of outcomes. Phoenicia is now highly profitable, the in-plant safety record has been vastly improved, and senior management has an exceptionally positive relationship with the unionized workforce. Phoenicia is now a great place to work, a good citizen in its community, and highly regarded by its customers (more about Phoenicia in Chapter Thirteen). This latest example has only reinforced my deep conviction that "it's all about who."

Too often, organizations retain B-level people because they haven't understood the profound difference between what is acceptable and what is possible. They think they're doing well when their team wins most of their games, but I want my team to win the championship. The difference between the best and a runner-up often is that the number of A's exceeds the number of A's on the other team. The New York Yankees come to mind in baseball because over decades they were managed by a great leader, George Steinbrenner, who understood the power of A's. As much as I sought out A's, it's clear now, with the wisdom of hindsight, that I settled for too many B's.

When you hire a Herman Eigen, you get a multiplier effect. Leaders who are clearly A's attract and make optimal use of employees who are also A's. In fact, A-level professionals will not work for long under leaders who are not A's. Excellent leaders attract excellent followers, and as a team they are more likely to contribute to organizational excellence.

The problem is that there are too few A players to go around, and they are greatly in demand. The result? You have to fight harder because of the inadequate supply of A's. However, to attract and retain A's in your organization, you have to create a great place to work. To hire and keep A's, you should have an organization that is attractive to them. This is something you build over time to increase the likelihood that you'll recruit and keep your fair share of A's. What does your organization have to look like to attract A's?

1. You have to pay attractive (but not unreasonable) salaries which demonstrate that you're willing to pay A players what they deserve.
2. You have to decide to create a work environment that is attractive to A's. You start with a culture where people are treated with respect and where there are agreed-on values that ensure high integrity and generosity toward one another.

3. You ensure that your company is a meritocracy where excellent performance is identified and rewarded, and there is a commitment to professional growth on the job.
4. You create a program of symbolic gestures which demonstrate that you always think about your employees. I have used such small personal benefits as subsidized lunches, soft drinks and snacks, and health club memberships. With each small perk, you're sending a positive message to everyone.

How do you distinguish A's from B's? There's not a lot of science to this process. Obviously, they must meet your expectations in regard to intellect, values, passion, work ethic, and experience. Their assimilation into the organization is also critical, and should be carefully planned. Once they are inside the organization, I constantly ask myself four key questions about them:

1. Do they respond to challenges in a creative way?
2. How deeply committed are they to the pursuit of excellence—to raising the bar?
3. Will they push back? Can they honestly and openly disagree?
4. Finally, are they highly promotable?

Let me explain how I think about leadership. It's possible that you have someone in a job who is doing reasonably well—and is a B. But you know that an A player will do more and will constantly seek to raise the bar. If you're getting twenty-two miles on a gallon of gas, you're looking for thirty. The A player will frequently exceed expectations for the job, generally by delivering more than what is asked for. Having almost unlimited upward potential is a key part of being an A player. That person is constantly growing. Only great people build great institutions.

Watching how a person responds to challenges is a key piece of the puzzle. You can see initiative, strong reasoning power, creativity, and a commitment to perfect execution, all of which add up to the pursuit of excellence. There is an anxiety to reach perfection. One can sense the level of commitment and how deeply A's care. They simply care more. They expect more of themselves.

A-level players are always striving to be the best they can be. An A-level employee is willing to take more risk. I'll give you an example of a lack of willingness to assume risk. We once employed a lawyer who would refuse to stick his neck out. He would identify a course of action and then explain the advantages and disadvantages of doing it or not, always leaving the choice to us.

We nicknamed him "suitcase versus briefcase" because he would not tell us which alternative was better. When I would ask, "Well, what would you do?" inevitably, his answer would be, "On the one hand, you might do this, and on the other hand, you might do that." An A player is willing to stick his neck out and, over time, will generate a higher batting average.

Leaders struggle to get honest feedback. All too often, subordinates seek to please the boss and not to disappoint him. A subordinate who agrees with you all the time is by definition not an A because this person will not be a sufficient agent of change. A-level players, in contrast, will generally push back when they feel it necessary, but will do so diplomatically. A typical response is, "Have you thought of doing it this way, Mort?" A's are too smart to say things like, "That's dumb. It'll never work."

My deep belief in the potential of outstanding performers and their ability to accomplish extraordinary things means that top leaders must always pay attention to hiring A's and retaining them. Increasing the number of A's should be a continuous process in every organization. For this reason, we take performance reviews seriously.

As an example, at Parkwood Corp., it's not uncommon for differences to break out over the performance rating a leader wants to give an employee. All performance reviews are shared two levels up before they are approved. That's to ensure that we build honesty and objectivity into the process. For many, there's normal resistance to telling staff about any negatives, so we plan this out carefully. Some things require a discussion, not merely a cursory comment.

We also always separate—by a week—performance reviews from salary reviews. The reason? People won't listen with the same intensity to a performance review if they believe there is also going to be a conversation about salary. You can't get their full attention. They are more focused on how much or how little money they'll be getting. With us, the salary review is put off for a week so that the conversation about performance can be serious.

• • •

Although one person's A's may be another's B's, sharing the understanding that there are A's, B's, and C's is important because it makes hiring and retaining a major discipline.

The secret of building an organization filled with A's is commitment, the will to act. It's not enough to say you want to hire and retain A's. You have to completely commit yourself and your organization to doing it. You have to make it your highest priority. You have to make clear to every senior person on your staff that organization building is his or her primary concern. If you do this well, your managerial staff will be the most valuable asset on your books.

CHAPTER 3

Building a Rich, Deep, and Ethical Culture

WE HAD SPENT THE BETTER PART OF A YEAR TRYING TO WIN A CRUCIAL CONTRACT. Just to compete for it, we had to invest almost $50,000 in studies and presentations and rack up hundreds of hours of management time. But if we won the deal, it would be our largest contract ever—a multimillion-dollar windfall at a time when the typical order averaged $150. We had thousands of customers then, and most of them spent between $2,000 and $10,000 a year for our products. So there was no mistaking the importance of this deal.

The contract was with one of the country's large industrial manufacturers, a brand-name company everyone knows. Finally, Bob McCabe, then our vice president of product and merchandising, came back from a business trip with the outcome. We had been approved. The contract was ours. The executive who gave him the good news, however, had added a footnote to the deal. He told Bob, "I forgot to tell you that we have an agent we work through, and the agent gets 5 percent of the deal."

We felt that the executive was asking for a side payment, possibly a bribe. It was tough news to hear. "Bob," I told him, "you know we don't do that."

He completely understood. We didn't have an agonizing discussion on the deal. There was disappointment, even anger—but not temptation. It took us one second to decide. This was a deal for which Bob had spent weeks of his time over those many months. Yet all we talked about was how we were pulled into spending all this time and money trying to win a deal we would never accept.

I knew the last-minute request was wrong—wrong for me, wrong for the company. We weren't going to touch it. Without a moment's hesitation, we walked away from what would have been the largest single contract in our history. If we made an exception, it would have changed the character of our company forever.

From our earliest days, one of our goals for the organization was to provide leadership of great competence and integrity, to always do what's right. It was part and parcel of our culture to treat our customers and each other with respect, fairness, decency, and integrity. I say it to my colleagues all the time: always do what is right, and always treat others the way you want to be treated.

An ethical culture starts with the person at the top and how that person lives out the values he or she teaches. I have never forgotten how deeply impressed I was at a meeting at West Point on leadership when I learned how the Army develops its leaders. Just three words are stamped on the cover of the U.S. Army's leadership manual: "Be-Know-Do." The Army advises emerging leaders that the most important of the three words is listed first— Be. How a leader lives out a commitment to ethical behavior teaches more than spoken words or printed words. It's not what you say. It's what you do.

I have a cardinal rule, and that is never to abandon principle. In the long run, you'll always do better.

Is this maturity or wisdom? Something I got from my mother? I know that my mother was as ethical as anyone I have ever met.

She drilled into us a simple yet enduring phrase: "Right is right, and wrong is wrong." She told us that if a hungry man sits next to you and asks for a piece of your sandwich, you are to give him the whole sandwich and never just a part of it. When I was growing up, I always thought there was one sure way I would die: if any of my teachers had sent home a note that I was disrespectful, my mother would have "killed" me over that lack of courtesy. She surely would have "killed" me for doing anything dishonest.

For years, when my brothers and I would be confronted with an ethical issue, we often would ask ourselves, "What would Ma think about that?" We knew that if any issue came even close to the edge of an ethical lapse, Ma would have frowned on it.

I've had very few ethical disappointments in my life. In business and in life, people are subject to all kinds of pressures that can compromise their values. We simply did not cut corners. The kind of people who have helped build our company and our foundation are people like us.

I've always held myself to high ethical standards. However, just saying you want behavior that meets the tests of integrity and fairness isn't enough. Just putting values on a piece of paper isn't enough, either. Enron had its code of ethics. So did WorldCom and any number of companies that have fallen into severe trouble due to ethical lapses.

Building a positive ethical culture starts with hiring the right people and putting values high on the list of hurdles needed to get into an organization. Every leader has to then take an active role in clearly communicating his or her ethical expectations to employees. I've used very clear language that all our employees can easily understand. You are only as good as your actions and your word. Warren Buffett said it well: "Lose money for my firm and I will be understanding. Lose a shred of reputation for the firm and I will be ruthless."

We've also put in place clear written standards—read and discussed regularly at numerous management meetings—and a process for enforcing those rules. A leader must understand, interpret, and manage the corporate value system. There needs to be constant communication by leadership about the rules of behavior.

Being scrupulously honest is enlightened self-interest. It extends to how you deal with all outside contacts as well. Even the practice of gift giving during the holidays has become a burden that in some ways is inconsistent with the spirit of holidays and contrary to the philosophy of building sound business relationships with customers and suppliers. Our policy is unambiguous and straightforward: we discourage all gifts, no matter how small or large. If a gift from a customer or a supplier cannot be returned graciously, it gets sent to our human resources department, which will raffle it off to our staff. We thank the givers for the intention, but note that our corporate policy forbids us from accepting any gifts.

I once read that a culture is more than pleasant surroundings and good working conditions. It is mostly the way we relate to each other—the extent to which respect, fairness, decency, and integrity are all found in our daily business life. I thoroughly believe this and refer to it frequently.

JoAnn White, our program director for the Mandel Foundation, puts it this way:

> The moment you walk through the door, you can absolutely feel the difference. Over the course of the past thirty years, I've worked for several employers. This is the best organization I have ever worked for, and it's because of the people here. The culture puts a very high value on respect for each individual. There are no politics. There is no pecking

order. No one overlords over anything here. People who have the title of vice president behave like any other member of the team.

Everyone who works for Mort is extremely intelligent and very professional. So the result is you have a group of people who come together to just do their work—not play games to gossip or figure out how to get ahead at someone else's expense. When you walk in here, you immediately feel as if you are part of a team which will do the best possible work it can that day, that week, that month. And everyone is all very proud of the work they do.

It's because of the culture that Jack, Joe, and Mort have created. Mort Mandel gets his own coffee. He doesn't expect anyone to get him coffee. What does that say to you about a man who is running multiple companies and doing wonderful work in the world?

There are subtle ways that a company can respect its employees. I'll give you one good example. We have a lunch program here under which a local restaurant is chosen every quarter. As an employee you can order lunch at a discounted price. Part of the cost is picked up by the company, and the lunches are brought here so you don't have to leave the building if you don't want to. Just the fact that Jack, Joe, and Mort thought about what could make our employees' life less complicated and simpler is a sign of respect and appreciation.

Over the course of my life, I've learned a great deal about how to create an ethical and positive culture. Treating others with respect, kindness, and consideration can make a big difference. If you want to be number one with your employees, they have to know and trust that they'll be number one with you—and that starts with how you treat them. Through trial and error and much reflection, I've put together a set of basic responsibilities for each member of our management team that allows every leader to live out our culture every day. These guidelines cover personal conduct as well as our dealings with each other. I believe in every one of them.

Personal Conduct

1. Maintain a positive, optimistic attitude—one that enthusiastically promotes the welfare of the company and its staff. Your enthusiasm will transmit itself to other people.

2. Familiarize yourself with company policy and support it at all times. Never criticize the organization, your boss, or any policies to your subordinates or to anyone except your boss—and then don't just criticize: try to present constructive suggestions for improvement.

3. Jealously guard the good reputation of our organization.

4. Act as though individual, group, and company morale are your basic responsibility. Examine every action you take to make sure it will improve—not hurt—morale.

5. Never jump to conclusions on the basis of flimsy or partial information—particularly when it can affect an individual adversely. GET THE FACTS. Always get both sides of every story.

I learned this last principle the hard way. Many years ago, I hired a young person who was habitually late to work. Every week, it seemed, he would came in later and later. One day, he arrived four hours late. I was upset. I saw him come through the door and immediately confronted him.

"What's going on?" I demanded. "Do you want to keep your job? This is ridiculous. You've been coming in late on a regular basis, and now you're four hours late."

Finally, I took a breath to give him a chance to answer.

"My mother died this morning," he managed to say calmly.

I felt as if I had been hit by a ton of bricks. I recovered enough to tell him I was so sorry for his loss and also sorry for confronting him the way I did. I quickly learned a lesson in how important it is for a leader to ask questions first, make sure he or she's getting both sides of every story, nail down the facts, and shoot later. The incident led directly to rule 5.

6. If you don't know the answer to a question, tell the person asking that you will find out the answer. This never hurts your standing or authority. Giving the wrong answer can hurt you and the organization. (You would be shocked at the number of sophisticated people who don't get this. I have more respect for someone who says, "I don't know, but I'll get back to you," than for someone who simply wings it and answers with a guess.)

7. Don't be indiscriminate with information that might be subject to misinterpretation or misuse. Respect your responsibility to protect confidential information.

8. Never discuss your pay or anyone else's pay with anyone except your boss.

9. Avoid any activities that could detract from a good business atmosphere. For example, do not drink alcoholic beverages during regular working hours, during lunch or dinner, or at any other time when the business of our company is involved.

Luckily, in the early years when we served wine and beer to employees at company dinners, we never had an employee who either injured himself or lost his life because of alcohol. But at one point, my wife, Barbara, and I took a vacation to Acapulco, Mexico, and became friendly with a vice president of a major airline. He told us the sad story of an employee who had too much to drink at a company event and then drove home to his family. He was involved in a fatal accident. From that day on, I understood why the airline banned alcohol at all company functions. The story got to me, and we immediately put in the rule that alcohol would never be served at any kind of company event (an extremely unpopular decision).

The rule was especially resented in Europe, where it is more customary to drink wine, often at lunch but always at dinner. I know that some of our European executives have never forgiven me for it—to this day. The French were appalled. So were the English. After we merged our company with British-based Farnell Electronics in 1996, I served on the board of the combined companies as deputy chairman. At my very first board meeting in England, over lunch, a row of wine bottles stood on the table.

"Malcolm," I asked the board chairman, Sir Malcolm Bates, "what's this?"

I pointed to the half-dozen bottles of whites and reds.

"Would you like a glass of wine?" he asked. I said nothing then, but after the meeting I explained my rule.

"I don't go for this," I told him.

"What am I going to use as an excuse to stop it?" he asked.

"Just tell them I'm the deputy chairman of the company now, and this makes me uncomfortable."

At the next board meeting, no wine was served. The point was made, even though it did not make me popular in the boardroom.

10. Learn how to administer all important systems and processes, particularly those affecting people. Two examples are the annual job progress review and the annual salary review.

All of these rules are spelled out in our management manual. Most of them are there because of a personal experience of one kind or another. In many ways, they are some of the lessons of my life. They are not merely words in a manual, however. More important, they are made real in the regular conversations among managers in the hallways and offices. They're read aloud at management meetings and discussed at length. They're regularly revised and updated or simply stated more clearly. In other words, these basic responsibilities of every manager are kept alive in a culture that lives them every day. And they address the factors that have led people in other companies to compromise ethical behavior.

We also have written standards for how we want the leadership of our company to engage with other staff members.

Dealing with Others

1. Treat each person as an individual, preserving his or her dignity and self-respect. For example, never criticize a person in front of others.

2. Give credit where it is due. Where appropriate, put it in writing. Don't try to grab the credit, even if it is yours. There is no limit to what we can do as a group if we don't care who gets the credit.

3. Focus on the positive behavior, the value, and the importance of our people. Most people can be expected to do a good job. Therefore, policies and practices should be based on trust and respect for the individual.

4. If something goes wrong, don't try to find out *who* is to blame. Instead, find the cause of the problem, with the objective of trying to correct the basic cause. Pinning the blame on a person does little in itself to solve the problem, and it may create bigger problems.

5. Exercise positive leadership by giving reasons for specific actions and by explaining and interpreting policies and practices. Never make statements like, "That's what the boss

wants." This type of remark will simply weaken the person making the statement.

6. Carefully measure the performance of each subordinate. If a person is not performing up to standard, blame yourself unless and until you have taken all steps necessary to help that person improve. It is your responsibility to help your staff develop themselves.

7. Evaluate people you supervise as fairly and as objectively as possible—being "protective" of them only hurts them, the company, and you.

8. Don't gossip, and don't accept gossip. The best way to do away with "rumors" is to give people the facts and reasons behind plans and programs.

9. Don't play favorites—control your actions so that they are impartial.

10. Recognize that only an individual's boss can give direct orders to, or reprimand, that person.

11. Don't place the blame on either your boss or the organization when you have to tell a subordinate something that you think will be displeasing. Doing so is unprofessional, and only weakens your position with your subordinates.

12. Communicate effectively—try never to surprise your boss or your subordinates. Ask yourself, "What should my boss know? What should my subordinates know?"

13. Invite and create opportunities for two-way communication with staff members. Establish an atmosphere where staff feel free to discuss work-related issues openly with their supervisor.

14. Every person has an ego. Handle it with care.

We've created these guidelines gradually over decades of experience, and they have served us extremely well. They are a part of creating and sustaining a positive ethical culture, a fair and decent workplace where people are treated with respect and dignity. So when an ethical issue pops up, like the one that cost us a multimillion-dollar contract, there wasn't even a discussion about what we should do. The answer was in our bones.

CHAPTER 4

What Happens When You Ignore Culture, People, and Values

IN THE FALL OF 1995, I received a surprising letter from England from a long-time acquaintance of mine in Cleveland, Robert Horton. I had gotten to know Bob, who had then been CEO of British Petroleum's North American operations, through the Cleveland United Way and other community activities. When he left that job and returned to England, he became chief executive of British Petroleum worldwide. Then I lost track of him.

Dated September 15, the letter began innocently enough: "Please forgive me writing to you out of the blue after all these years, but I wonder if I could explore a possibility with you." Intrigued, I kept reading. Bob, who by then was chairman of British Rail, said he was on the board of Farnell Electronics, which had identified Premier as "an obvious strategic partner."

I had heard of the company before and in fact had a file on them as an acquisition possibility, as I did for many other companies. But I was surprised to receive this unsolicited letter from Bob. He requested a private "meeting of the minds" to see if we had any interest in a discussion.

At the time, Premier was fifty-five years old. We had set earnings records thirty-four times in our thirty-six years as a public company. Our operating profit margins had reached an all-time high of 22 percent. In the fiscal year ending May 31, 1995, Premier's net earnings were a record $108 million on operating revenue of $818.2 million.

I had been chief executive of the company for more than four decades. I was seventy-four years old. My brothers, Jack and Joe, were eighty-four and eighty-two. Foolishly perhaps, I was starting to consider the question of whether I was mortal. We talked about the future every once in a while, but I was in no rush to leave a job and a life I thoroughly loved.

In fact, only a year earlier, we had come as close as you could get to buying another New York Stock Exchange company with greater sales than our own and half the profits. I believed we could bring that company's operations to our levels of profitability and make a huge success of it. We spent nearly four months of work and due diligence on the deal. I had taken an official photograph with the CEO of the company. A press release had been written to announce the acquisition. But at the very last minute, the day before the announcement, I cancelled the deal. I had come to believe that the cultures of our two companies were so different that the gap could not be bridged.

Even though the numbers, market possibilities, synergy, and benefits of scale made sense, I foresaw a culture clash that could jeopardize the success of the acquisition. In my view, incompatibility between cultures is the reason why many deals never realize their full potential. Culture—the people, the values, and the beliefs of an organization—can be far more important to the success of a particular deal than the numbers. Yet endless groups of investment bankers, lawyers, and accountants who are there to crunch the numbers give too little thought to that. They validate the efficiencies of bringing together two very different organizations, without sufficiently thinking about the impact on the people who make those companies living things. The result of all this "due diligence" is that when deals make sense on paper, that's enough for many of the people involved to turn on the green light.

•••

The letter Bob sent to my home was intended to rouse our interest—and it did. Only a year earlier, we had walked away from what would have been the biggest deal of our lives. Now, maybe Farnell was a company we could buy. Maybe they would want to buy us. So I wrote Bob and told him that we could meet in our office on my next trip to England.

Little more than a month later, on October 13, we were sitting down in a conference room for lunch at Premier's offices in Horsham, England, far from Farnell's headquarters in Wetherby, West Yorkshire. At the table was Howard Poulson, a tall, thin man who was fifty-two and had been recruited as CEO of Farnell two years earlier. Howard said the right things: he told me that he saw Premier as the best in the business and that our two companies would make a powerful combination. Bob was a big booster of a deal. They had no problem if I wanted to become chief executive of the combined company, though Howard said he wanted to stay with Farnell. All told, it was a get-acquainted meeting with few specifics. I left, thinking that perhaps something could come of this.

We kept in touch by phone and by private letters via fax until Howard came to New York a month later. On November 10, we had dinner at the Hotel Pierre on Fifth Avenue. Howard told me his life story, and it was not dissimilar to my own. He had grown up in a poor but wholesome environment, and his mother was very insistent that he get a college degree, which he did, at Imperial College in London.

At the time, I found Howard bright, modest, and easy to talk to. He was openly ambitious, but in what I believed to be a healthy way. He came across as a professional manager, someone who understood bottom-line management. He seemed to share our values, and he was not afraid of the full price we would be asking for Premier. That evening, we spent three solid hours talking about what a deal might look like. We agreed to pursue our talks, and I agreed to spend a couple of days visiting Farnell to get to know the company better.

Later that evening, I jotted down my observations of the meeting. My conclusion: "I liked Howard and I think he would 'fit' in the Premier environment. I suggested that he would be the logical choice for the merged company CEO."

Bringing our two companies together seemed to be the proverbial deal made in heaven. Our combined companies would create the world's third-largest and most profitable electronic component distributor and one that would have a blue-chip following in the investment community. We would have strong positions in North America and Europe, able to offer coverage to every type of customer. There was almost no market overlap. The merged companies would have considerable supplier influence and an enviable range of franchises. No less important, we thought the company would be capable of careful expansion into South America, Asia Pacific, and China.

Farnell was slightly smaller than Premier, $830 million in sales versus our $900 million run rate. Farnell also was considerably less profitable, $120 million in pretax earnings versus Premier's expected $190 million. Our market cap was then $2.1 billion. Farnell's was at $1.5 billion.

There were four ways to do the deal. Premier could buy Farnell, Farnell could purchase Premier, we could simply form a strategic partnership, or there could be a straightforward merger of the two businesses. I had no strong preference at the time, but felt that Howard really wanted to buy Premier and run the show. That was fine with me. By then, I had led the company as CEO for thirty-eight years and was now seventy-five years old. I hired investment banker Lazard, who assembled a team headed by Felix Rohatyn, Steven Langman, and Eitan Tigay. Together with Premier board member John Colman and chief financial officer Phil Sims, we formed a strong group to work on the deal.

The following month, on December 6, I flew to London with Sims to continue our talks. Our dinner at the Atheneum Club with Howard and Bob convinced me that we were well on our way to a deal. Bob said he felt that a combination of our companies was a natural and that the entire Farnell board wanted it to happen. The board, he said, would give us a "clean sheet of paper," so that all the members, including the chairman, would resign if that's what we wanted. He said the board believed that it could be "the deal of the century."

I told them we needed to craft an arrangement that would make our U.S. management team feel very positive about the arrangement, their own personal job security, and the new company's future as a business. Bob and Howard said they completely understood. If anything, they treated me with great respect and admiration, as if I were the boss. "What would it take to give you comfort?" they asked. It was almost like "Ask, and you shall receive."

Bob drove us back to our hotel, offering to take me through the Tate Art Museum any time, day or night, on a private tour. He seemed to be using every bit of his charm to make us feel wanted. He certainly succeeded with me. Bob said we could have dinner during his forthcoming trip to the United States in February, when he hoped there would be good news to celebrate. I then spent an hour with Howard in the lobby of Hotel Claridge moving the deal forward. It was my fifth meeting with Howard, and it was another good one. He showed great deference toward me—so much so that when I returned to my bedroom at the hotel, I sat down and wrote the following notes:

> By now, it appears as a given that he expects to defer to my general thinking on policy. He stated that his style calls for advance discussion of all important matters, and repeated his anxiety to communicate fully and well in advance so as to achieve consensus with me. He appears to feel that my experience and knowledge can be a strong asset and that he would want to take advantage of that. He hopes I am willing to invest "important time" in facilitating a full and total integration. I said I would do it for at least the next several years.
>
> He repeated again he just needed to know what I wanted. I mentioned the possibility of a title for me, and that I understood that the chairman should be a "Brit." I made it very clear I saw him as the CEO, noting his age of 52, versus mine, and that I saw my role as making him as accepted as possible by the Premier team. I felt I could work with him easily and comfortably, based on our discussions so far. He repeated the exact same set of feelings. He wants to be the CEO, but again will do everything he can to build and maintain a very harmonious relationship with me.

What remained to be negotiated was the price. The next morning, I met with Howard at nine in the morning, and we quickly came down to the basics. Howard said he wanted to do a cash and stock deal and proposed a formula for the price based on the current market value of the stock and a premium of between

30 and 50 percent. At the time, Premier stock was trading at $25, and the company's all-time high was slightly above $30. Howard said the starting point for any bid would be the current price and a premium on the high. He proposed $33 a share.

"I want to be fair," I said, "because Premier shareholders would own much of the new company." I proposed a "middle position" as a good compromise, and that the midpoint between a premium of 30 percent, which was $32.50 a share, and 50 percent, which was $37.50, was $35 a share, a couple of dollars higher than Howard's proposal. I told him I wanted to avoid any tension between the two of us and didn't want to haggle. I concluded that the fairest compromise for both sides was to move immediately to the midpoint, $35 a share.

Howard, in turn, argued that at $35, the deal would cost him $164 million more than he had anticipated.

"In a total consideration of $3 billion, that isn't a big deal," I said.

But the price issue remained unresolved. Instead, we agreed that the name of the new company would be Premier Farnell, with a U.S. headquarters in Cleveland and the corporate headquarters in the United Kingdom. We agreed that board meetings would alternate between the two countries. Howard said he wanted to keep the board at its current size with eight directors and would offer us two seats. In retrospect, this was something of a warning sign, because only the night before he had said that three or four Premier directors sounded okay.

Before leaving for the States, we agreed to face-to-face meetings once a month and a scheduled telephone call at the midpoint between meetings. I concluded that Howard was very anxious to do a deal, along with Bob and the Farnell board. This was now serious, very serious. We contacted Lazard and encouraged them to work on the deal.

Meantime, Howard and I kept in touch by phone. As is often the case in any deal, there are both practical and emotional issues that come to the surface. That became very apparent during a forty-five-minute phone call I had with Howard while I was in Jerusalem on December 19.

Howard seemed on edge. At the $35 share price, he said he was "very concerned" about how London's financial analysts in "the City" would react to the deal once it went public. Howard said the price, the American involvement, the new board, and our ownership position (we would retain a 25 percent stake in the combined companies) would raise eyebrows. He expressed concern over my request for three directors and the chairmanship of a board committee, saying that a chairmanship would require heavy involvement, and someone living in the United States might not be able to make that commitment. He obviously didn't know me.

There were other concerns as well. He was worried about finding the $50 to $60 million in profit improvements necessary to make the deal work and about the large transaction fees required to get the deal done. In my notes of our telephone conversation, I wrote that "Howard is nervous about me and whether he will have the authority as CEO to move the business and make decisions. He did say he expected to work closely with me, but it appears that as the days go by, he is becoming less likely to do so."

Nonetheless, our teams kept working on the deal. Howard came to New York on January 10 for a dinner at the Pierre Hotel, where we agreed to many of the final terms of the deal. We met in the lobby at 7:15 PM, went to dinner, where we had a pleasant, half-business, half-social dinner, and then proceeded to my apartment at the Pierre, where we finished up at 10:30 PM. Among other things, we agreed that as CEO Howard would not unilaterally fire anyone from the Premier senior management team of about sixty leaders without my approval for the first six months. I had spent decades finding and nurturing these leaders. I considered them essential to our success. It would be easy for someone unfamiliar with the team to make hasty and wrong decisions about people, which could badly hurt the company's future. So at my urging, Howard agreed that he would work through me or my direct reports on any employees he might consider "redundant" due to the merger. Where we might disagree, there would be a six-month delay so that Howard could learn why we disagreed. We shook our hands on those terms and met the next day at the offices of our investment banker to continue our work on the merger.

Ultimately, we agreed to compromise at $34 a share, reflecting a 39 percent premium over our market value, and I agreed to two seats on the board instead of three. When the details of the $2.8 billion deal were announced in London on January 23—twelve days after our evening negotiation—the Fleet Street press quickly assumed that Farnell was paying too high a premium for the merger. The *Financial Times* quoted several analysts who called the deal "incredible," "high-risk," and "fantastically brave." The worst coverage was yet to come. "The Lex Column" weighed in with a highly negative take that concluded, "The neatness of the industrial logic [of the deal] should not be allowed to divert attention from the financial risks . . . Howard has pulled off what he called 'a once in a lifetime deal' after less than two months of due diligence. Unless Farnell can do a better job of selling the deal, shareholders should vote it down at next month's extraordinary meeting."

The reaction immediately stung Howard. During a telephone call, he said that the value of the deal was a big problem. The media's declaration of a "premium price" was causing negatives and lots of pressure. I offered to help. I was eager to make the deal because I believed in it. My brothers and I would retain a continuing investment in the new firm, and I had confidence in Howard to execute the deal. When I next went to London to meet with Farnell's management team and Howard in early February, he seemed quite tired and even contentious. Howard kept repeating the need "to be realistic" and "practical." Much to my surprise, he also said "My job is on the line" and "I will be unemployable in London if the City is disappointed in me."

But the brouhaha over the price came to nothing. We were able to explain the value of the deal to shareholders and analysts alike. On February 15, exactly five months after Bob wrote and sent his first letter to me, 84 percent of Farnell's shareholders voted in favor of the deal.

The reaction from our shareholders and friends was highly enthusiastic. From Milton Metz, a shareholder and close personal friend from high school, who was with WHAS Radio in Louisville, Kentucky, I received this letter: "Since Premier is so much part and parcel of your life, I'm sure it's a bit of a wrench, with it all, to see your creation become someone else's. Don't think me overly sentimental about it, but even being a mere stockholder (and good friend) I got a little twinge out of the transaction . . . We liked the line drawing of you in the *Wall Street Journal*—not the look of a ruthless tycoon at all, more the visage of a kindly, aging futz with good intentions."

He wasn't the only one to ask me if it was very emotional to do the deal after all the years my brothers and I spent building the enterprise. The truth is, it wasn't, because the conclusion of the deal was a very positive experience for all of us. We got Premier to where we needed to get it. The deal made fifty-six of our top leaders millionaires, and would also make Jack, Joe, and me billionaires, able to use even more of our money to help the social sector.

Maybe it can get better than that, but it doesn't really ever get much better. It's like three scoops of ice cream. How much more can anyone eat?

But my elation with the deal was short lived. Two weeks before the merger was completed, Howard told me he could no longer honor the agreement we had made to protect the Premier senior management team. His argument was that the pressure from the City for quick results required him to deeply cut costs.

"I've got to do something," he insisted. "Otherwise, I'm not going to be employable."

"Does doing something mean breaking your word?" I asked.

"I can't help it, Mort. I've got to do it."

I was not merely disappointed. I was totally frustrated. We had agreed to these terms. We had shaken hands on them. We both had a set of carefully written notes, the content of which we both had agreed on. Where I came from, that meant something. It obviously didn't mean enough to Howard.

Perhaps Howard did not see this as "breaking a promise." Perhaps he felt he had no other choice. After all, this was not a formal, legal agreement.

Very sadly, when those cuts would eventually be made, I would have no say in any of them. Howard's team literally took out their pencils and crossed out the names of some of the best people on our team because their compensation was deemed too high. There was a reason they were highly paid—they were worth it. They were among the best people in our employ, and they loved the company. What I had spent the better part of my life building—an organization filled with people of exceptional quality, passion, and values—Howard was getting ready to destroy even before the deal was legally completed. In all, more than a third of the top 150 executives would be fired.

Two weeks before the completion of the deal, I saw a handwritten list of the cost reductions made by Howard's chief financial officer. He wanted to cut out too much of the brains. It was shocking. I felt betrayed.

To some extent, I blamed myself for what happened, because the terms Howard and I had agreed to privately were not part of the board-approved contract. We had thoroughly discussed them, written the terms down on paper, and shook our hands on them. I mistakenly thought that was enough. Clearly, it wasn't, and clearly, Howard felt tremendous pressure to cut costs sharply and at once.

Despite my disappointment, I wanted this deal to get done. I was committed to doing everything I could to help with the transition. I had meticulously planned a three-day tour of Premier facilities for Howard and meetings with management and employees. We would have a 7:30 AM breakfast in Cleveland on his first day of the trip and meet with my senior management team. I had arranged for a private plane to bring Howard and me to the key facilities in the United States. We would go together to answer the questions employees or managers might have about the merger.

Over breakfast, on this first day, Howard asked about the plans for the day. I told him I would introduce him to the company's top management team of about a dozen people and then we could meet with them and answer questions.

"I don't think you need to be there," he said. "Come and introduce me and then leave after ten or fifteen minutes."

"Are you kidding me?" I asked. "Could you please explain that to me? I'm going to introduce you at nine, and I have the whole corporate management team there."

"No," he said tersely. "You really don't need to be there."

So I walked into that first session with our top management in the room, introduced Howard, and then walked out. No doubt, the people in the room were shocked. They knew I was supposed to be there with Howard for three straight hours. Instead, I was gone within five minutes. I imagine that by three that afternoon, all of Premier's senior people worldwide had heard about this abrupt change.

Over the course of all our meetings leading up to the deal, Howard had led me to believe that my knowledge and experience were strong assets and that he wanted to take advantage of them. He knew of my deep concerns about our senior management team and their job security. And he had agreed not to dismiss a single member of that team for the first six months without my agreement. Now, all of that went out of the window.

I learned one thing: a board should ratify any agreement that is ever made in a corporate setting. Perhaps shaking hands has become obsolete—not in the world I live in, but sadly in the wider world. Shaking hands isn't useful unless both sides have the same values. That is a hard-earned lesson.

Despite my early optimism about the deal, the truth was that Howard and I had very different approaches to managing a business. I was focused like a laser on hiring and retaining the best people and on achieving operational excellence by diving into the details of the business. Howard, in contrast, was fixated on deal making and satisfying the analysts in the City. John Colman, who had helped take Premier public years earlier and was a longtime board member, had a good view of the differences. He was the other Premier board member with a seat on the Premier Farnell board of directors. He sized up the situation very well:

> The British and the Americans are two people separated by a common language. The two cultures are quite different. And the cultures in the City of London and Wall Street are quite different, although London at that time was becoming infected by some of the go-go tendencies emerging on Wall Street.

The focus was short term. Poulson was afraid that if he missed his projection by even one pence per quarter, he was headed for the guillotine. The driver for Poulson was size and earnings per share. It was "Give the City what it wants." There wasn't much strategic thinking about real opportunities. Always his focus was on what are they saying about us, not on what are we going to do and why.

Poulson got himself into a box because at the time of the deal some analysts were saying that he was overpaying for this American unit. He came to believe the only way he could pay off the debt he incurred was to cut, so he cut hard. He cut out some real talent in the American operation, some of the best people. One of Premier's best operating executives was an Asian woman who could really make things happen. She was let go. Nobody in his right mind would have come to that conclusion. Everyone else would have said, "If I want to create a global business, this is potentially one of my major players."

The Premier people were really shaking their heads. That was the climate, and that was manifest early on because Poulson felt he had to make certain numbers. This is the Wall Street–City of London infection.

It went downhill from there. For the first six months after the deal was completed, earnings failed to meet expectations—despite the cuts that Howard made. We rarely said anything to each other even though I sat in the boardroom as deputy chairman, a director, and the largest single shareholder in the combined companies. As the earnings faltered under Howard, not once did he ever come to me to ask a single question. In fact, he came to Cleveland at least four or five times and sat in offices not much more than twelve feet away from my own on a floor with only a half-dozen offices. He never came by to say hello to either my brothers or me.

Howard was fired less than a year after the deal closed. I personally led the charge. At the board meeting where that decision was reached, every eye turned to me. Then we discussed who would be the interim chief executive.

"Mort, would you do it?" asked Sir Malcolm Bates, the non-executive chairman of the board.

Bates was as dedicated as any board member, a true English gentleman with no airs. The former chief operating officer for the U.K. General Electric Co., he was a superb executive and a ray of sunshine. We would develop a warm friendship over the years, and I felt privileged to know him.

"I'm finished," I said. "No, I really don't want it."

Then, board members started a discussion about how much they would pay me as an interim chief executive until a search firm could find outside candidates for the job. It was clear that I was the only person in the room who knew the business in detail, and the post would be a temporary one. Finally, I agreed to do it— without compensation, only expenses.

"I'll do it because it's the right thing to do as a director," I said. "But I need one full day to think about it, and tomorrow I will tell you for sure."

I wanted to make sure I could coax Bill Hamilton, who had been our Premier president and was then serving as a consultant to the combined companies, into doing the job with me. After the board meeting, I went back to my hotel room in London and immediately called him.

"You say yes, and I'll tell them I'll do it," I told Bill. "You say no, and I'll tell them I won't do it. "

"I would like that very much. When do you want me over there?" he asked.

"Tonight," I replied.

There was a long silence until finally he said, "Tonight? It's already 2 PM here."

"Bill, please get on an airplane and come straight over," I said. Another long pause occurred.

"Okay."

He landed in London the next morning, and we immediately flew to Manchester and then went to Leeds to visit one of Premier Farnell's largest facilities. One British newspaper announced the change with this headline: "Grandfather Takes Over Premier Farnell." Over the next eight months, until a new CEO was found, I tried to restore hope and confidence. I brought back several terminated executives. I changed a few division heads. One role I took for myself, especially in the United States, was to give "pep talks" to middle managers to urge them back on track. Another role was to meet with the London financial press, which for the most part felt deep skepticism about the financial aspects of the merger. But the truth was that Howard had lost a lot of the value in the deal by trying to placate a few analysts in the City.

About two-and-a-half years after the deal closed, we sold our 25 percent interest in the company and took a 40 percent haircut on our shares, a loss of some $200 million, because the stock price never recovered. All told, I stayed on the board for five years before leaving for good.

The lesson? The soft stuff counts. People, culture, and values bring competitive distinction. Yet almost all deals are put together on the basis of numbers, market possibilities, synergy, and the perceived benefits of scale. Too little consideration is given to people, culture, or values—when it's those very ingredients that determine whether a deal will truly pay off over the long term. Instead, often the investment bankers, lawyers, and accountants validate the efficiencies of bringing together two organizations by identified cost reductions and possible market expansion, with too little attention to culture fit.

Those early decisions exacted a terrible cost. By firing many of the people who made it possible for Premier to be a superior company, Howard lost much of the know-how, the discipline, and the energy and creativity of a high-performing organization. By rejecting a culture that had perfected customer service and had pricing down to a science, he lowered Premier's profit margins to the same level as Farnell's.

In any organization, or in any merger, it's often the so-called little things that make a difference. It turns out that the little things, if not well executed by the highest-quality people, aren't little things at all.

CHAPTER 5

What I Learned from Peter Drucker

THE FIRST TIME I SPOKE TO PETER DRUCKER WAS BY TELEPHONE. It was the mid-1960s, about five years after we had taken Premier Industrial Corp. public. I knew very little about Peter at the time and was calling him not for management advice but rather as a reference for a candidate I wanted to hire as a consultant.

He answered the phone himself, with one of the most distinctive voices I had ever heard. Every word was spoken slowly and in a measured way, with a heavy European accent that I would later learn was Viennese.

"Peter Drucker here," he said.

I quickly introduced myself and then asked what he thought of the investment adviser candidate who had named Drucker as a character reference. Apparently, Peter had some of his own money invested and was satisfied with the person's performance. As it turned out, the purpose of the telephone call became a side issue. I asked what Drucker did, and he explained that he was an author and a management consultant to companies.

He was then teaching at New York University, taking a public transit bus into New York from Montclair, New Jersey, where he lived with his family. He had written a dozen books, had consulted with the leaders of IBM, General Electric, General Motors, and many other well-known companies, and had become the premier management consultant of his generation.

I was hungry for more insight and wisdom, especially advice on how we could achieve higher growth in profit and revenue and how we could develop our people to handle that growth. We had done extremely well since going public, with five consecutive years of record profits and revenues. I knew we could do better, and I was striving to raise the bar to improve the performance of the company.

Peter impressed me immediately. Though I was a complete stranger to him, he was gracious with his advice and generous with his time. By the time our telephone call was over, I was not only convinced to hire the investment manager; I also asked if Peter would take us on as a client. His reply: "With pleasure." We agreed to meet in New York the next time I had to be there for business.

I'll never forget the first time I actually met with him, because while I was completely dazzled by his mind, I also was distracted by some of his personal habits. For our first session together, we met in New York at the Harmonie Club on East 60th Street. We sat across from each other, with Peter resting in a high-backed chair, with a large open briefcase at his side on the floor. He must have had a dozen bottles of various kinds of medicines in the case. During our meeting, he kept bending over, reaching into the briefcase, and pulling out one medicine after another. He put drops in his eyes. He popped some pills. Not once did he ever stop talking or listening. I concluded that he had to be a classic hypochondriac. To be honest, I found his behavior disconcerting at first, but after a while I didn't notice it at all—all I noticed was his absolute brilliance.

Over the years, Peter would become one of the most influential people in my life, a friend and a mentor. He was a great thinker who possessed the most penetrating mind of anyone I had ever worked with. I ended up becoming very fond of him. He was just a lovely guy: cheerful, sociable, diligent, and challenging. Yet, mostly, it was his clarity of mind and thought that really sold me on him. Over the next two years, I would meet with Peter every month for a full day of consulting. During those sessions, I felt as if I were sitting at the feet of a master teacher who was always enlightening and often enthralling. I can say we sometimes disagreed on things, but Peter never failed to make me think more deeply about people, leadership, and management.

In 1999, Drucker told a journalist for a local business magazine, *Inside Business,* that he recalled my sessions with him as if they were last week. "There were three things about Mort that always stuick with me," Drucker said.

> The first is the absolute integrity of the man. Secondly, he's one person who knows how to do an acquisition successfully. Ninety percent of acquisitions misfire, you know. But 90 percent of Mort's work in acquisitions has been successful. The reason: he knows what to acquire and how to acquire— and then how to run it after the acquisition. The third thing is that he and I hit it off so to speak with our mutual interests in the non-profit world. We, Mort and I, very quickly came to realize that we shared this interest, and he has been exceedingly successful with his social programs, his non-profit work.

Always, there was the same routine. I would write him a letter about what I wanted from our next session. We would meet and then he would write a long, single-spaced memo about our day together. These letters were wide ranging in content and thought, filled with personal asides, intelligent observations, and smart ideas and lessons. Peter could be incredibly self-deprecating and humble. After a meeting in early February of 1970, for example, Peter wrote: "I am struck by how much ground we covered, albeit rather thinly. And the summary of our day, which I promised you, is therefore likely to be quite a bit longer than I had thought at first. I am about to leave for South America and want to get this off to you—and this then means that I have not had time to work on it enough to make it brief. But I hope that this will serve your purpose, even though it is not as good as it should be."

Over the next five pages, Peter would distill our talk to its essence, never too shy to render a strong opinion, even one I might disagree with. What was most striking about Peter was how he could see your business in high-concept terms and draw important conclusions about it. He noted that we had spoken about what businesses Premier was in and what we should be in. He wrote,

> Our conclusion was that your main business concept is to identify areas in which tradition conceives a business to be product-focused whereas it actually is market and service-focused. And the businesses you look for are businesses which supply what I would call "intermediates" of production and distribution, that is, critical ingredients which, by themselves, have a fairly low unit cost but which have a very high value in terms of the functioning of the system to which they are being supplied . . . These "intermediates" cost practically nothing compared to the damage or loss their absence or malfunction would represent. If, therefore, you organize their supply in such a way as to be able to guarantee performance, the value you contribute to your customer is way beyond anything you might possibly charge, which gives you both

profit margins and market opportunities way beyond anything
a product-focused approach could ever see or exploit.

In just a few sentences, Peter articulated our entire business
philosophy and profit model. He reaffirmed for me the idea that
you could earn considerable profit by delivering superior service
on important parts that could cost very little. For me, the big
question was how to best organize the company and the people in
it for the best possible performance and rapid growth. Drucker
said, "I think we agree that 'entrepreneurship'—that is, the capacity to see new business opportunities beyond those you are exploit-
ing today—will be a function of top management so that the
question is not just how one builds entrepreneurship into the businesses but also how one obtains a few more people who can move
into this top management function. And this led us to the whole
problem of basic organization, and especially organization for
maximum growth."

Peter urged me to meet regularly with the "second- and third-
level people" in the business and ask them: "What do we in top
management have to know about your work, the company, and
the market? What opportunities do you see for Premier? Where
do you see dangers and vulnerabilities? And altogether what questions do you want to ask us? What ideas do you want us to think
about?"

I used Peter's advice all the time, incorporating much of it into
my leadership style. Every place I went, I would make what we
began to call "Howdy Rounds"—the phrase actually came from
General Motors, and the idea was to meet and greet the rank and
file in a plant or office before you would meet with the management. I always disliked the idea of executives who parachute into
a plant or office, quickly walk past everyone to make a beeline to

the executive offices, and then shut the door. A Howdy Round told people I cared about them and what they did. It made me accessible. I respected the people who worked for us and greatly appreciated their efforts on our behalf. Almost always, I picked up valuable ideas from people on the front lines of the business where information was less likely to be sifted and filtered for senior leadership. Frontline employees would give me the kind of feedback that often revealed hidden challenges or led to quick improvements. If you're not in the trenches often enough, you'll never be able to get execution exactly right.

It's why every military general should spend some time in the field of battle, why every sales manager should periodically take out his or her sample case and call on customers, why a social sector leader should get out of the office to spend time with the people his or her organization is serving. In every instance, you see a picture of reality that can give you a deeper understanding of your business.

Peter also suggested that I take an inventory of our top twenty people, listing what they have actually done well and in what areas they have potential or performance capacity. "The most important thing," he wrote to me, "is to make sure that the major opportunities are staffed with your best and most productive people rather than try to worry about staffing everything perfectly—which no one has ever been able to do."

When I think back on all my sessions with Peter, I have to say that this is one of the most valuable pieces of advice he ever gave me. Fairly quickly, Peter sized me up as one who so completely loves the details of work that I can get too deeply involved. "You try to protect your people and worry a great deal about what they cannot do," Peter wrote. "Yet it is clear from your record that you must have an extraordinary number of people of very great performance capacity—a disproportionate number indeed. And so it might perhaps be better to ask what your people can do and simply take for granted that even a very good person rarely can do with real excellence more than one thing—one then has to supply what he lacks some other way, and one usually can do it."

The more I got to know Peter and the more he got to know me, the more confident he became in giving me the kind of feedback a CEO rarely gets from others. I brought Bob Warren, then our executive vice president, with me for a meeting with Peter in May of 1970, at which time we reviewed the top twenty people in our company. Bob tells me that even today, more than forty years after the fact, the memory of that meeting lives with him:

> I remember it like it was yesterday. Peter was a brilliant man, absolutely brilliant. Peter said to us, "You guys have the best-run company for a small company I have ever seen."
>
> We were telling him about our dissatisfaction with one vice president. And he looked at Mort and said, "How many Bob Warrens have you hired? How many do you think you're going to hire?"
>
> Mort said, "They are very rare."
>
> And Peter said, "Then, you are going to have to deal with the B players and the C players because you can't always find the A's."
>
> In effect, he said you have to deal with people who are not perfect. We still looked for great performers, and we usually found them. But I would say that Peter's message made us a little more flexible.

The inevitable problem here is that the supply of A's is too small. So if you want to fully staff your organization, you must use B's but fight hard to keep the C's out. Without B players, most organizations would shut down. Nonetheless, Peter was impressed with the quality and depth of our senior team. They were A's, after all.

In a letter dated May 11, 1970, he wrote:

You did not express a single reservation regarding a man's character, his basic integrity, or his dedication. And while you may be somewhat optimistic and suffer slightly from the syndrome "he is my boy," which you diagnosed in some of your associates, this is still the kind of weakness you would notice and would have registered. One can live with weaknesses of knowledge, of skill, of experience, and of temperament—in fact, one has no choice. And one can put a man to productive use if he has the dedication, no matter what his limitations are in this or that area of knowledge, of experience, or of skill. This is, therefore, a very strong team. In fact, it is an exceptionally strong team, I would say.

At our session at the Harmonie Club and in his follow-up letter, Peter had a fascinating point of view on an issue that I often focused on: the ability of people to appraise others. I found that managers are likely to overrate people. Drucker was adamant that this is a fundamental problem in management. "You expect people to be good judges of people," he told me.

But that is exceptionally uncommon and cannot be expected. You pointed out that your "appraisals" do not bring out the important features and, in particular, they do not bring out what a man does really well and what he, therefore, is likely to be able to do. But in an organization which, like yours, depends so very heavily on individuals rather than on a system, this is crucial. My first conclusion, therefore, would be that you do need both a system that enables you to know what people actually do in performance rather than what opinions about their performance are—that is, a system which records performance against pre-set expectations—and a system of promotion under which decisions about people are taken seriously and are discussed at considerable length, with no one person making a final decision by himself.

We followed Peter's advice, but I have to say that getting completely honest performance reviews is a near impossibility. Why? Because by and large, reviews are done by nice people who find giving an honest but critical review extremely difficult. Rarely do people want to tell the blunt truth; they generally want to deliver positive news. People don't like to criticize people, and they don't like to fire them, either. So you're always swimming upstream when you try to put in systems that honestly appraise people. At Premier, we had highly placed people review every performance report for all our managers. At least two people—not just the direct supervisor—had to sign off on every report. It brought us closer to the naked truth, but never as close as I would have liked.

Another area that Peter called an "important vulnerability" was my own heavy involvement in the business, along with Bob Warren and Bill Hamilton, my two key direct reports who were in charge of operations. This was especially true after we acquired Newark Electronics, our Chicago-based distributor of electronic components. Peter wrote,

> You have to spend a great deal of time trying to understand these businesses and can, in effect, not really give direction. You either have to leave it to the general manager and hope that he knows what he is doing. Or you have to become yourselves managers of the business which, at once removed and long-distance, is not done well as a rule, apart from putting far too much of a strain on your very short resources of time . . . I do not, let me say, believe that one management

can manage everything and anything. I have no use for the conglomerates, as you know, and consider them monstrosities which will fall down under their own weight. But within what one might loosely call industrial supplies . . . your expertise should carry you.

Bill, then executive vice president of Premier, also remembers that session with Peter:

Mort was very self-confident of his own abilities and his style of leadership, but was always open to new ideas and critiques of his ideas and style. There were only a limited number of writers of business books for whom he ever expressed real respect. The primary one was Peter Drucker, whom he brought to Cleveland to talk with our top managers, something that he had not done before and, if my memory serves me correctly, was never done with any other management consultant.

While Bob Warren and I both participated, the conversation was primarily between Mort and Peter. Peter took the lead in most of the discussions, with Mort showing great respect for his opinions and replies to topics brought up primarily by Mort. I would certainly characterize it as a discussion between a highly talented pupil and a highly qualified teacher whom the student highly respected. It was meant to be a learning session and an evaluation for possible future presentations to the Premier executive management group in Cleveland. Mort treated Peter with great respect, and Peter showed the same respect for Mort. It was an informal setting with no preplanned agenda, somewhat of a different approach from meetings planned and held by Mort.

Mort referenced items from Drucker's books in some of his presentations to managers as a part of our programs designed to improve management skills. I believe we trusted what Drucker wrote and felt it was right for us and for our managers. I know Mort read and carefully absorbed all of Drucker's books as a part of his own process to improve his own skills.

Peter was a great listener, and his observations from listening hard to people were very valuable. He raised significant questions over whether we had enough A-level talent at the top and at the next level of management. In retrospect, I have to say he was absolutely right. Even though I surrounded myself in those days with a top team—all A players, including Bob Warren, Bill Hamilton, and Phil Sims—too often, we accepted B players in lower but still important jobs. That put far more pressure on the A players in the organization. Looking back on my sessions with Peter, it seems he was right on target with this observation.

As Peter put it to me, "I have learned not to allow my race horses to carry all the load they are willing to carry, simply because that very rapidly takes the last trace of 'race horse' out of them. You are putting a very heavy burden on very few people—maybe you have no choice just now; but watch out lest you ask more of them than they can give, or that anyone can give, for a prolonged period."

Truth is, we *were* putting a heavy burden on people. We believed in both sitting in the ivory tower and also walking in the trenches—we weren't doing just one or the other. We were leading and managing our company, and we were deeply engaged in the details of that business. Today, I'm still involved in the details. I still believe in that; I teach it, both to my business associates and to philanthropic organizations. As it turned out, the A players around me were able to handle the workload and, in fact, thrived on it. And yet, had we employed still more A's, we would have done even better. I realize that now.

Peter's remarks raise an important issue: How involved should a leader be in the details of the business? There are no magic formulas. It reminds me of the time my wife, Barbara, wanted my mother to show her how to make my favorite cookie. It was a square, flaky concoction, with crushed walnuts and sugar sprinkled on top. As my mother mixed the ingredients in a bowl, Barbara kept asking her how much of this and how much of that. My mother didn't use measuring spoons or cups. It was a pinch here and a pinch there. Her experience in baking cookies over a lifetime guided her judgment. The answer might not have fully satisfied Barbara, but it speaks to the question Drucker was getting at. As a leader gains experience over many years, he instinctively knows how deeply involved he should be in the details. The boundaries change based on the existing conditions.

The conventional wisdom on delegation in management is that (1) you hire a highly capable person, (2) you orient that person to your business, and (3) you let that manager do the job his or her way. Conventional wisdom often adds a postscript: give the person six months to a year to perform. If the results are good, you don't get in the person's hair. You leave the manager alone. If the results are poor, you fire the manager.

That's not my style. It's not how we helped satisfy tens of thousands of customers. It's not how we helped shareholders send their children to college or buy a second home, or created fifty-six millionaire employees at Premier. And it's certainly not how we were able to touch and influence the lives of so many with our philanthropy.

If I owned a restaurant, I would be in the kitchen every hour tasting the food. I wouldn't taste every dish. It's about sampling, putting an occasional fork or spoon in an appetizer, an entrée, a dessert before it goes out to the dining room. It's about the view, sizing up the cleanliness of the kitchen floor and tables and the uniforms on the employees.

But I wouldn't stay in the kitchen. I'd spend fifteen minutes of each hour there, and forty-five minutes out front with the customers, making sure they were wowed. When they walk into my restaurant, I want them to see a place that is attractive, welcoming, and clean. It has to be a place where they want to be, an environment that makes them feel pampered and comfortable.

You sell three things in a restaurant: food, service, and atmosphere. A restaurant is the sum of those parts. It's how Starbucks can charge $3 for a cup of coffee when McDonald's charges $.97. Take away the service and the atmosphere in a Starbucks, and the company would have to sell a cup for the same price as McDonald's.

It's not how much you do or how much you delegate. It's what you delegate and to what extent. To my mind, you don't ever delegate strategy or execution more than 95 percent. On this point, I disagreed with Peter, but what I loved most about him was that he told it like it is. There was no sugar coating on his insights, no hesitation to give you his honest opinion, no matter how you felt about it. His thoughts on delegation and overloading my senior team were examples of issues we just didn't agree on.

Still, we spent a lot of time together discussing what exactly top management should do in an organization. Almost always, Peter would throw out one gem of a thought after another. After yet another meeting with him at the Harmonie Club on August 12, 1970, we explored how decentralized a company such as ours should be. Peter believed that you could only decentralize and turn over to other people what you yourself can understand. "It is a misunderstanding that decentralization results in lessening the power and authority of top management," he wrote a week after our meeting.

> The true aim is the exact opposite, that is, to make top
> management stronger and more capable of doing its own, the
> top management job, by relieving it of all things that other
> people in the organization can do . . . In a large and diversified

business, top management no longer can really do everything. It can indeed "do" very little. It either encourages people to do things their own way and focuses on results and standards only. Or it is forced to turn over more and more of the work to carbon copies, that is, to people who imitate. And carbon copies are generally weak and get increasingly weaker. In fact, it is a sound rule—both General George C. Marshall and GM's Alfred P. Sloan, who certainly did the best job in judging men I have ever seen—never to promote a man who does things the way you, the boss, do it, never to consider it praise of a man that he is "very much like myself." This is really condemnation. The greatest praise for a man in a large and diversified organization is "I don't understand how he does it and couldn't do it this way myself; but he gets splendid results." This is a man who is doing his own work and doing it himself rather than depending on the boss and aping the boss.

Frankly, I fight for people who do share our values, our work ethic, and our passion. I don't consider them clones or puppets. I do want people who can stand on their own two feet and run an organization. But that doesn't mean the person shouldn't be anything like me.

Such leaders generally pick up our standard operating procedures. Much is spelled out in writing and constantly revised for change and upgrading. Years ago, a new CEO took over Avis, the car rental company, and immediately announced that he was throwing out all the policy manuals because they were stifling. My answer to that is, "What if the policies are helping you achieve net profits of 10 percent after taxes? Would you still throw them out?" I don't agree with either extreme. Who wants a person who copies everything you do like a puppet? Who wants a person who does the exact opposite of everything you do and doesn't share your values or your ideals? It's never either extreme. In all my years in business, we sought to acquire companies with existing leaders who generally did not understand this conversation. To me, that spelled "opportunity." Such leaders do not understand the magic combination of superior people and superior execution.

Peter also was a big advocate of getting into the trenches of a business and, in particular, communicating with and managing frontline people. He wrote:

> I would strongly suggest that you ask each of the men who report to you, and in turn the men who report to that first top layer of management, to give you in writing first a statement of the results you and Premier should hold the man and his component accountable for, with a clear indication of the priority tasks—with a deadline. You then should also ask them to tell you what the factors are, both in the market and environment and within the business, on which his success and his economic results primarily depend. This is, incidentally, the best way to come to grips with the question: "What is our business and what should it be?" Insist on something well thought through. And when you get it, sit down with the man and spend a lot of time on it, trying to understand what he is trying to tell you, but also trying to identify the areas where you and he see different needs and opportunities. And when there is a difference, try to apply to yourself the rule: "the man is sane and he means well, and therefore a difference such as this is likely to mean that he sees a different reality than I do, and possibly a reality that is just as real and better than the one I see."

We continued our sessions until Peter moved to Claremont, California, in 1975. In a letter to me on September 15, 1975,

Drucker said, "I moved to Claremont primarily for the climate—or rather because Mrs. Drucker began to enjoy eastern winters less and less. But as for myself, I came to Claremont to be able to work more. New York's distractions interfered with work."

We stayed in touch for many years, though our consulting sessions ended. For a long time now, I have hung on the wall of my office one possession I greatly prize. It is a reprint of an October 14, 1996, *Forbes* magazine article about Peter in which he named me as one of three business leaders he very much admired, along with Jack Welch, CEO of General Electric, and Andy Grove, CEO of Intel. I couldn't believe it. Peter went on to say that "Mort Mandel only acquired companies that made sense and meshed with [his] product line." It was a great honor for me.

What did I learn from Peter?

He helped me understand that it is a leader's job to identify the stars, personally, and to watch over them closely. Strategy and management development are the top priorities of the chief executive. Top management, he thought, must find ways to interface with lower levels of the company and spend time with the brightest managers, asking them to define problems and opportunities, and learning their strengths.

Peter was always insistent on putting your best people where the biggest opportunities are. He also thought you needed to develop a feeling of responsibility in key people so that they can help draw the blueprint for the future.

After all my sessions with Peter, I created this list of his thoughts and ideas:

How do we grow at a faster rate? Make sure all exceptional growth opportunities are led by your best people.

How do we set priorities? Find the difference between projects that build, and projects that merely eliminate sloppiness.

How can we improve people's ability to judge other people well? Very few people can do this alone—do not expect it. Instead, install a group system to make it happen.

How do we manage a wide range of businesses? Determine the key factors for success in each business unit. This must be done by the general manager, which means this is a "must" skill in order for a manager to be a true GM.

How do we improve our appraisal system? Have at least two persons doing the appraisal and record a person's performance against preset expectations.

How do we build entrepreneurship deeply into a management group? You can't. Only top management can do this. When you find people with these interests and talents, move them into top management.

Why don't many managers grow faster? Perhaps you keep their jobs too small and don't distribute enough responsibility.

What is top management's role? Deciding what business to be in; people decisions in depth; allocating capital.

How do we spot very high potential managers? Meet in structured but informal settings, with a mix of lower levels of management. Ask, "What do you think I need to know about your job; what do you see as opportunities? Problems? What should we in top management do that helps you? Hinders you?"

I've taken these lessons to heart and teach them everywhere, just as Peter so convincingly taught me. Our sessions together mattered to me as few other things in my life did.

CHAPTER 6

Killing Yourself for Your Customer

LET ME TELL YOU A STORY. It's one I tell often because more than almost any other story, it describes why our company became so successful. Through the years, there were many other stories like it, but I'm especially proud of this one because it completely captures the essence of flawless execution.

At 11 AM on a Saturday in 1990, a representative from one of our biggest customers, Disney, called our Orlando branch office. The phone was answered even though the office was closed, because we had twenty-four-hour coverage, seven days a week. A major amusement ride at Disney World was down. Disney wanted to know if we could get them a part needed to get the ride up and running. Our representative on the phone called our warehouse in Chicago.

That part was immediately picked off a warehouse shelf and driven to O'Hare airport for a 2 PM flight to Orlando. In Florida, the salesman on the Disney World account met the plane at about 4 PM, jumped into his car with the part, and called Disney to let the park know he would arrive there in less than an hour. At about 4:40 PM, he pulled up to the gate, where they were waiting for the

69

part. A Disney mechanic installed the part within minutes, and the ride was up and running at about 5 PM. Total down time? Roughly six hours.

Disney had feared that it would take until midday Monday to get that ride back in operation. So, instead of actually losing six hours, the company assumed it would lose a couple of days. Disney estimated that the downtime on this equipment would have cost it about $1,000 an hour. Bottom line? We may have saved our customer as much as $20,000 by responding so quickly and flying a $42 part from Chicago to Orlando and then having a salesman drive it straight to the park on a Saturday afternoon.

Two weeks later, our branch manager in Orlando got a phone call from a senior executive at Disney.

"I have your invoice for $42," he said. "I know what you guys did. Send me an invoice for $500 or something. I'm embarrassed that you're not charging us enough for what you did."

Our branch manager responded, "You are a valued customer. We send you many shipments during the year. Most of it goes through smoothly, and we make a nice profit on it. When you need us, we're there. And we don't charge extra for that."

How many times do you think this executive at Disney told that story? What do you think happens when someone walks into Disney and says, "I know you're buying your parts from Premier. Whatever you are paying, we'll give them to you for less." He most likely would turn that person away. That is the value of awesome customer service.

What I love most about that story is that it was a natural outcome of training, culture, and leadership by example. We drilled customer service into our people. We told them again and again: "Kill yourself for your customer." We put it in our mission statement. We focused on it in training sessions. We discussed what it meant in meetings with leadership. Some of our employees used to joke, "Now, you don't mean you want me to shoot myself?" And I would say, "No, but close."

Superior customer service applies to all organizations that serve people, whether they are hospitals, nonprofits, or multinational corporations. As we all know, customer-focused organizations are unfortunately all too rare. We know this because all of us have waited on the telephone for half an hour or more to get a human voice, only to find that the person couldn't solve our problem anyway.

Awesome customer service is an idea that is easy to state but more complicated to live by. Amazon knows this. So does Southwest Airlines and Zappos. The facts are that if you take care of your customer, you'll do better. What set us apart was how that commitment changed our entire approach to business. We listened to our customers and used what they told us to make things better. We created a culture dedicated to service and found that there is a strong link between good employees and happy customers. More specifically, it meant that if a product was in our catalog, we always had to have it. This implied that we had to perfect our inventory management so that we could deliver a part quickly to a customer who needed it quickly. And to do that, we had to be always available, seven days a week, twenty-four hours a day. Customers will pay for that kind of service, and too few companies can deliver it because it requires flawless execution.

For every Disney story, we have dozens more, such as the time we chartered an airplane so that we could deliver badly needed fire hose to the West Coast for an active forest fire that was raging out of control. Our customer never forgot it. Or the time the Navy hospital ship *Mercy* was docked in San Francisco, preparing to sail to the Persian Gulf after the outbreak of Operation Desert Storm.

The *Mercy* couldn't leave port because it needed to replace a part in its fire extinguishing system. On a Friday morning, the Navy called a distributor of ours in San Francisco, who did not have the part in stock and called us immediately. We were able to ship the part the same day.

A few days later, however, the *Mercy* left the dock and began to take on water. We received another urgent call at noon on the following Wednesday for a part—a water siphon—that was not in our inventory. It had to be custom made on our machinery. We stopped certain work in the plant, retooled some machinery to make the part, cut it on the machine, and then put it on a plane for delivery the next day. The *Mercy* was able to set sail for the Persian Gulf to care for war casualties not much more than twenty-four hours after the telephone call. Our distributor never forgot that.

Long before superior customer service became a part of the business conversation, we believed in it. We did it. We understood that there were mainly two ways to sell things: on price or on service. Price is the first refuge of all merchants: How cheap can you sell it? It's a wonderful business approach if you can be good at it. Walmart proved that. They found a way to sell on price, and they are extraordinarily successful and profitable as a result. But few companies have the power to go to their suppliers and ask them to reengineer a product so that it can be sold for less. And fewer companies still are able to get the volume on an item that makes slim margins add up the way Walmart does.

So if you sell on price, you probably won't do as well. The profit margins are usually paper thin when you run a business on price. But a good margin in a business is what gives you room to pay competitive salaries and invest in improvements. If you buy something for nine cents and sell it for ten, you have precious little margin for error. That's an uncomfortable place to be.

I know because that's how my brothers and I started out in 1940. We sold auto parts on price. We'd walk into a garage or repair shop and ask the owner if he needed spark plugs or lug nuts or tail pipes. Inevitably, he'd ask, "How much?" And just as inevitably, we'd answer, "What are you paying now?" If he said 72 cents for a spark plug, we priced ours at 69 cents. If he said 77 cents apiece, ours were sold at 74 cents. We sold most spark plugs at 69 cents each and paid 67 cents to get them. A little math will tell you that there wasn't much profit there.

We were just cheaper than anyone else. We were frustrated by this and saw no future for ourselves down this path. Sometimes our customers simply turned us away with, "I don't want any spark plugs, kid." And then something that proved to be very profound happened: we decided to ask our customers, "What parts are you having trouble getting?"

One of the first answers to come back was moulding clips. In the 1940s, just about any car being sold had chrome strips along its sides to give it a sharper look. The chrome was attached to the car with a moulding clip, no larger than a thumbnail. Moulding clips were sold by part number. But very few people knew the long, complicated catalog numbers on such parts. It required locating a parts catalog and figuring out which listed part (if you could find it) was the one you needed. For the average garage owner, that was a real nuisance. It was too much. My brothers and I spotted an opportunity.

In the late 1940s, about 90 percent of the cars on the road were Fords, Chevrolets, or Plymouths. So if you had moulding clips for each of those three brands, you pretty much covered the needs of your customers. That's exactly what we did. We found a source for clips from a jobber in Kentucky and then went to a small bar next to our store in Cleveland to get three empty cigar boxes, one for each major car brand. We dumped the parts out of the boxes they came in and put them inside our cigar boxes. We tied each part to a little string with an inch-square tab and put our own simplified part numbers on them. The Ford box had parts with numbers like F1 and F2. The Chevy box had its C1 and C2 parts. Then we went into the field.

Our sales pitch was simple. We opened up the box and said, "Henry, do you need any of these?" And guess what Henry did? He fished around, perhaps picked one clip and recognized it. "Yes," he says, "I can use some of these. How many are in a box?" At first, we would decide on the spot whether to say twenty-five or fifty. We had no rules on how to package them yet. We'd take the order, write down the part numbers, and go away.

The question they would almost never ask: "How much do they cost?" We were stunned.

We settled on standard quantities in each box and began to test different price levels. Back then, we paid about 6 cents a clip. We tried selling them for 8, a 33 percent markup. No problem. We tried 9 cents. No problem. Within three months, we knew this 6-cent clip could be sold for 10 cents. We went from small margins, selling on price, to margins that would fuel growth and expansion selling these hard-to-get items.

We had found a need and filled it! From that time in 1947 forward, that single idea helped define our business future. By the time we added our tenth specialized product family, we realized that this approach *was* our business. Systematically over a year, we found other needs—from sheet-metal screws to high-tensile-strength nuts and bolts that would last longer in use—and began to get rid of the products that everyone sold on price. Within two years, we threw out 70 percent of the low-margin items and were busy converting our product line to specialties. Our profits skyrocketed. But more important, we had hit on the idea that took us away from price.

At the end of the first year, we hired a mechanical engineer to go out and engage our customers to find out what else they were having trouble buying. He brought back dozens of ideas, and we managed to obtain our share of these hard-to-find items that would allow us to obtain above-average pricing.

From the day in 1947 when we understood the power of "to find a need and fill it," until April of 1996 when we merged our company, almost fifty years later, we never changed our basic business approach. In each of our divisions, we always tried to find out what our customers wanted but had trouble getting, and sought to add those hard-to-find items to our product line.

We were always reaching. As our business expanded, we always asked ourselves how we could do better. It never occurred to us that now we had the money to buy ourselves a boat or other expensive toys, or that we could take more time off for leisure. Instead, we focused on building our business. We were systematic about the ways in which we constantly reviewed the basics of our business, seeking out opportunities in the marketplace.

This sensitivity to "find a need and fill it" relates just as fully to philanthropic endeavors. It is a mind-set that focuses on the uncovering of new needs. Whether we see the need for a new product in our business or a new feature in a Mandel Foundation program, we react the same way. It is this relentless search for important unmet needs that characterizes our work. We are committed to creating ever-higher expectations and creatively striving to realize them.

Providing awesome customer service was the next giant step. We now had the profits to do more for our customers: carry discontinued parts they wouldn't be able to find elsewhere, keep more parts in inventory, doing whatever it took to satisfy a customer. Find a Need and Fill It and Kill Yourself for Your Customer became the two commandments of our culture. Over time, our customers became convinced that they could count on us—and that realization helped us hold both our margins and our customers.

Many companies talk customer service. Too few companies really deliver on it. Few companies have a deep and serious conviction about service. Most companies see their service as "important, but good enough." Delivering superior customer service does not fire them up sufficiently to invest extraordinary amounts of time and money to make it happen. That's why I believe one way to differentiate what you do is to create a business model that includes superior customer service. Any organization that devotes itself to fully satisfying a customer is really in the business of exceeding expectations.

What makes superior customer service hard to provide? There's often pressure inside companies to sell on price. People in sales are often eager to discount prices to close a sale, not realizing that those discounts can also diminish an organization's ability to invest in such features as superior customer service. When we acquired Newark, the electronic parts distributor in Chicago, our core beliefs were put to the test. It had been a company that sold on price. We had to transform it into a company that sold on service. Bob Warren, who was then president of Premier and who completely embodied the values of our culture, played an instrumental role in that makeover. Bob remembers:

We were a company that believed in selling specialties, not commodities. We believed in solving a customer's problem instead of just pushing product out there. We put the emphasis on service and quality. That was a key factor in the growth of our company. Our goals included being very profitable, not pushing solely for volume.

Sometimes it was hard to convince some of our salesmen of these goals. We simply fended off the pressure to cut prices and discount. Mort and I are both highly disciplined people, and we hired people who could function under that discipline. You have to be disciplined and you have to be tough to make these results happen.

The most important decision that we made after the acquisition of Newark was the modest repricing of the products based on our improved customer service. We decided giving customers better service was worth more. We first tested it in Minneapolis where we had an executive who had exceptional knowledge of his customers. The customers were used to getting price discounts. We had to retrain them. We actually increased our prices by small amounts. It was selective and varied by the product. It gave us more margin, and we did it logically, by product line, not across the board. We knew the products and the expectations of the customers. We rolled the increases out over a six-month period and thus changed Newark from a company that sold its products by discounting prices to a company that delivered great service and quality products to its customers. Our customers truly appreciated this, and our profits were impacted very positively.

Why didn't other companies do it? It's hard to change a company's culture. If you have a sales force trained to get sales volume, it's difficult to train them to operate the way we did.

One of the happiest moments of my life was when our company became the lead anecdote in a *BusinessWeek* cover story on customer service called "King Customer." I still remember the cover date: March 12, 1990. It was the media's acknowledgment that companies that listened hard to their customers and responded quickly to their needs saw their bottom lines thrive. The story went on to describe another Disney-like situation. Early one afternoon in late 1988, we received a call from a manager of a Caterpillar Inc. tractor plant in Decatur, Illinois. A $10 electrical relay had broken down, idling an entire assembly line. This time, our sales rep found the replacement at our Los Angeles warehouse and rushed it to a plane headed for St. Louis. By 10:30 that night, the salesman on the Caterpillar account had delivered the part, and the line was up and running. I believe that transaction cost us several hundred dollars. We billed Caterpillar $10, but like Disney, the company would never forget it.

The prominent mention of our company in an article filled with names like IBM, Coca-Cola, and Intel knocked my socks off. It warmed my heart. Plenty of other companies were featured in the report, from American Airlines and DuPont to 3M and Ford. But we had so completely delivered on our pledge to provide superior customer service that the writers made us the lead story. They put us front and center. To us, customer service is our main event. Killing ourselves for our customers was part of our path to success.

CHAPTER 7

Principles Make a Difference

MY MEETING WITH BERNIE MADOFF OCCURRED ABOUT A YEAR BEFORE HIS NAME SPLASHED OVER SO MANY HEADLINES IN SO MANY NEWSPAPERS. Introduced through a good friend, we met in the library of my Palm Beach home for an hour and a half. His investment fund was closed to new investors, Bernie told me, but he would consider taking our money.

For years, I had heard friends tell me of the steady returns they were routinely getting on their money with Bernie. When the market was up, they made a bundle. When the market was down, they still made out. One year, they received perhaps a 14 percent return; another year, perhaps 12 percent; another, 17 percent. There was never a loss year. It was just enough to speak to your greed, but apparently not so much that you identified it as greed.

One of my friends, who ran a feeder fund channeling money into Madoff's firm, would tell me at least once a year to look Madoff up. He suggested he could pave the way and get Bernie to let me in as a direct investor. Although Bernie and I were both members of the Palm Beach Country Club, we didn't know each other. So I finally agreed to a meeting.

I expected to be dazzled by him—and yes, he dazzled me. Bernie was as smooth, sophisticated, and knowledgeable about investing as anyone I had ever met on Wall Street. I was not only impressed with Madoff; I enjoyed the time we spent together. He had an awesome CV, with lots of notable experience on Wall Street and in the financial markets. And at our meeting, Madoff did everything exceptionally well, at first making it clear that he wasn't looking for money and then, after getting to know me, suggesting that he just might make an exception.

"Well, you know Bernie," I said, "all we need is some transparency."

"No, that's my stock in trade," he replied, "and I am not going to tell you how I do this."

"It's pretty hard for me to understand why you wouldn't tell an investor how you've been able to make these returns," I said.

Bernie, however, wouldn't budge.

To be completely honest, I was torn. Longtime friends and associates had been urging me to put our money into Madoff for what seemed like forever. They had been telling us of their substantial and remarkably steady returns year after year. The evidence—at least the returns they experienced—was compelling. But I had put together over the years strict guidelines for our investments, and Bernie's firm violated two important ones: the need for transparency and the requirement that a fund be audited by a first-rate auditing firm.

Madoff did not meet these basic standards. It was not about his values. When I met him, he passed my personal tests. He was smart, sophisticated, likable, and obviously highly successful. But he didn't pass our policies for transparency and the requirement of an auditor who had immediate credibility.

So I turned Bernie down. After all, I had spent a lifetime putting principles into the rule book. What would it say to the organization if I neglected to follow my own principles? Two weeks before he was charged with securities fraud on December 11, 2008, I had lunch in New York with a close Madoff associate who again urged me to put money into Bernie's fund. As it turned out, investors would lose billions from the fraud. Our commitment to principle saved us millions.

I tell this story not to brag about how we resisted Bernie Madoff's charms but rather to explain the importance of policies and procedures to the pursuit of excellence in an organization. In business, written, enforceable policies provide comfort and direction. They unite all the members of the firm, allowing everyone to work in harmony with one another. Policies give you consistency.

When it comes to leading an organization, managing individuals, or picking an asset manager to invest money, policies and procedures are vital if you strive for flawless execution. This isn't about building bureaucracy. Too often in today's business world, policies are portrayed as handcuffs for creativity, innovation, and speed. Nothing could be further from the truth. Smart policies not only save you from the Madoffs of this world but liberate you because they help people act on their own without higher management approval. If it's within the box, you decide. If it's outside the box, you go to your boss. Policies let your employees more clearly understand the boundaries. If you have clear policies and believe in them, there is a stock answer for the challenges that occur most frequently. There's a measure of security and liberation in that.

Discipline is one of my best friends. What made Premier so successful and what differentiated us from our competition was, in part, the quality of our execution. The same is true of the

Mandel Foundation. That takes discipline: a structured, organized system to which there is 100 percent adherence and fidelity. People have to get that. Striving for perfect execution, setting a high bar for yourself and your organization, is all about discipline.

I learned this in the military during World War II, when I ended up in Officer Candidate School and became an officer in the Medical Administrative Corps. My role was to relieve doctors of certain administrative responsibilities so that they would have more time to take care of wounded soldiers. Quickly, I became aware of how unsystematic I was in my daily life. I saw what happened when things are planned, when there is structure and a commitment to values. I was not well organized when I went into the U.S. Army at age twenty-one. When I came out four years later, I was a different person. I learned process. I learned systems. I learned the value of system discipline.

The armed forces have an intense commitment to discipline, execution, and system fidelity. U.S. Army manuals are many inches thick. There is a procedure and a policy on almost everything, from making a bed so tight you could bounce a quarter off it, to marching troops in close-order drill. The Army tells you how to clean a gun and what to do about sore feet. Over the years, the Army figured out how to do pretty much everything. This is why it could effectively train hundreds of thousands of troops, move them around the world, clothe and feed them every day, and put them into battle. I was in awe of the efficiency of that system. The Army systems worked. When there wasn't a regulation to follow, the commanders then stepped in.

When you understood that system and followed it, it made life easier. On a superficial level, my clothing drawers went from mixed up to neat. On a more profound level, that military exposure positively affected the rest of my life. When I returned home to our auto parts business after the war, I created a "Golden Rulebook" of our own guidelines in a three-ring binder. Years later, our efforts to seek flawless execution are based on procedures that institutionalize the ways leaders manage their organizations. Today, when new people join us, they're sometimes surprised because our process is so structured. But after a while, they get used to it. When things run like the proverbial Swiss watch, the people in the system achieve a better result.

Early in our business careers, we always asked ourselves, "How do we get to the next level?" Experience gained on the journey up the mountain was always put down and codified in guidelines and policies so that we could spread the learning through the organization we were building. In many companies, so much experience remains in the heads of the people who get the learning, and then it stops there. That's why I believe it's important to commit the core learning of an organization's leadership to written, visible rules and guidelines that can inform future decisions. There is no need to reinvent the wheel every day if you write things down.

People have the brains and the hearts to get this, but you can take your organization up another notch by making sure the ideas are ingrained in the company. As a leader, you're given the organizational clay to sculpt something that can be gorgeous and beautiful. It's up to you to take advantage of that opportunity. A commitment to flawless execution will change you for the rest of your life.

We've spent a lot of time developing policies for everything we do, from coaching subordinates to motivating others, from how to answer the telephone to how to serve clients. The guidelines are regularly revisited and discussed. Our management policy manual alone is divided into fifteen separate sections. Our investment policy manual is twenty sections long and provides guidance on everything from how we evaluate potential new asset managers and perform due diligence on a new fund to when we terminate our relationship. We have policy manuals for the Mandel Foundation as well.

What does all this attention to detail get you? A level of efficiency that is otherwise much more difficult to obtain. When we hired Jim Fox, who had been a Six Sigma black belt at General Electric, to become deputy director of investments at Parkwood Corp., I asked him to look into whether we could benefit from the quality system that had brought billions of dollars of productivity improvement to GE. I had long been an admirer of GE chairman and CEO Jack Welch and was intrigued by the savings and higher profit margins he achieved with the program. If a quality initiative could have such a dramatic impact at GE, where it led to increased operating margins of 18.9 percent from 14.8 percent, perhaps it could be of equal benefit to us at our private trust company. Six Sigma quality translates into having fewer than 3.4 defects per million operations in a manufacturing or service process. That is a remarkable level of perfection. I'll let Jim convey the story:

> One of my initial projects when I joined Mort's private trust company, Parkwood Corp., in 2005 was to evaluate whether we should implement a Six Sigma program here. So I did a mini-consulting study for Mort on what types of projects we might use Six Sigma on, how we would train people for it, and what impact it might have on the organization. At the risk of getting my black belt designation revoked, I came to the conclusion that we didn't need it. In many ways, Parkwood already had an emphasis on the pursuit of quality, without calling it Six Sigma. The Mandel way of doing business led to near zero defects, control charts, and rigorous control processes. Those kinds of things have been part of the culture that Mort and his brothers have practiced for decades. So I

recommended that we not pursue Six Sigma. Mort would pride himself on knowing that he didn't need to pay consultants to get that level of efficiency. To him, it was just common sense. It's the Mandel way of doing business.

There should be little or no variation on a theme. McDonald's and Coca-Cola are two highly successful organizations that have benefited greatly by adhering to policies that provide remarkable consistency across borders. You can go into any country of the world and order a hamburger or a soda and feel reasonably confident that what you got in Cleveland will be almost exactly the same in London or Paris. That is the efficient result of policies and procedures that guide exactly what McDonald's and Coca-Cola do in every setting.

Every idea doesn't have to be your own. When I come across valuable articles or essays, I often toss them into the manual. Why? Because they reflect learning of a different kind that all of us can benefit from. For example, there's a study from the U.S. Chamber of Commerce on employee job satisfaction. It shows that managers rank compensation, job security, and promotion as their top three paths to satisfaction at work. But it's a significantly different case for your basic worker, who first wants to feel appreciated, then feel that he or she is "in" on things, and finally feel that the organization is sympathetic and understanding about his or her personal problems. Understanding the needs of your employees is crucial learning. So we threw this into the management policy manual for all of us to think about all the time.

I believe that there should be a rule, guideline, or policy for pretty much everything a well-run organization frequently has to do—mainly because it makes "doing" easier for everyone in the organization. It's being clear about what we do and why. With us, people are drilled and trained in these ideas, and, as a result, we can more easily delegate important responsibilities to them. At the same time, and very important, we give our managers and senior leaders the flexibility to adapt and change our policies and procedures. When a guideline doesn't fit the situation, our managers are authorized to adjust our policies on the spot, right then and there.

At our Parkwood monthly management meetings, I'll often have members of our team read aloud from the policy manuals we've created. This gives me, or anyone in our senior leadership group, the chance to explain why we do it this way, to reinforce the accepted behaviors in the company, and to continually define our culture. In other words, it makes the rules real—not just words written on pieces of paper and filed away in binders to be ignored.

When it comes to investing money, for example, Parkwood does not just select investments. We mainly select investment fund managers. Our analysts spend important time thinking about what to buy and even more time thinking about who to buy with. Again, the policies let us focus on the "who" rather than the "what." We'll meet with a potential fund manager and go through a series of standard questions based on our policies: What keeps you up at night? How are decisions made? Who are your top people? If a bus hit you, who would step up? And our rules demand that the CEO of the fund must personally meet with me, as Parkwood CEO, before we commit. If not, we pass.

Why? When all is said and done, investing is a people business. So picking the right manager to invest with is all about who. The best insights come from one-on-one meetings with managers who like and trust you. It's important to understand the leaders and their motivations. So there's a detailed set of questions we ask all investment managers: Precisely how much of your net worth is invested in the fund? Who owns equity in the firm? Have the key partners worked together before? For how long? What seniors have left the firm, and where did they go? Can we talk to them? Is there an experienced chief financial officer? Who is your independent auditor? For how long with the firm? Because of the importance we place on values and integrity, we will never invest with a manager if there are any concerns regarding character.

Now that didn't come up with Bernie when I met him. But the policy book told me we had to pass. The truth is, I was sorely—but not sufficiently—tempted to make an exception. After I presented the opportunity to our investment committee a few weeks later, some members urged me to invest with Madoff anyway. One adviser said that there comes a time when you should make an exception to the rules. I decided, however, that leaders have to lead and that abandoning principle would set a poor example. My decision was that we would not invest with Madoff. I'm glad we didn't.

Principles make a difference.

CHAPTER 8

Factbooks: Key to Personal Discipline

I'VE ALWAYS APPROACHED BUSINESS THE WAY A CLASSICAL MUSICIAN READS A SHEET OF MUSIC. What counts is how well and how passionately you execute the notes as written, not how you improvise them. Whether you play the violin in a symphony or lead a for-profit or nonprofit organization, great execution requires discipline and focus. You cannot achieve flawless execution without a painstaking devotion to the details. It is not easy to keep track of all the things necessary to achieve such flawless execution.

That's why every manager I work with has a factbook. It's a three-ring binder that breaks down a manager's tasks into small, manageable steps. Such a factbook keeps you on top of the details and assures that there are no misunderstandings between managers and their subordinates.

At its simplest level, the factbook is a tool that keeps you focused and disciplined about your work. It contains the minutes of meetings with your boss, all assignments, your progress against these assignments, and a twelve-month schedule of future meetings. If it's put together carefully, the factbook is the place to go where your work life is both organized and crystal clear.

So when I work with a colleague in regular planning sessions, typically once a month, my three-ring binder has the same tabs as he has in his. The tabs quickly get you to the minutes of the last meeting, a person's prioritized assignments, and an update on what he's accomplished since our last session. Each task stays on that assignment list until complete. Nothing is forgotten. That makes it easy to focus on the important things and never lose your place. Every assignment is there in black and white, staring at the person who is responsible for getting it done. He can't forget about it. Just as important, the boss can't forget about it, either. Too often, that's exactly what happens.

All of us can get overwhelmed with things to do at work and in our lives. We're often racing from one meeting to the next, from one city or country to another. Every business is a fairly complicated system. If you're leading an organization and seeking flawless execution in the pursuit of excellence, the best way to stay on top of all the details is to have a clear accounting of them. The system reminds you of what's important. It also imposes accountability on the boss and the subordinate to get things done.

A factbook can take away excuses. Using this process, it's unlikely that people will not have enough work to keep them busy. And if a subordinate feels unhappy about something, the regular sit-down meetings with her boss gives her an opportunity to address these feelings. Mostly, the factbook can be the place where the details of your work are made the focus of how you do your work.

Generally, I am quite involved in the details. As the leader, I believe that typically you get what you inspect, not what you expect. Most often, when managers join us from other companies, that company has not had an intense focus on the details that lead to high-quality execution. A factbook makes this possible. It provides visibility to all the things that need to be done. It's a way to stay on top of the details.

To an outsider, a factbook looks deceivingly simple. To me, the three-ring binder that every key employee has is not merely a notebook. It is a process. Every month, almost every key manager in our company has a factbook meeting with his or her boss. Typically, it's a one-to-two-hour opportunity to have a thoughtful and candid conversation. Together, the manager and her boss review the progress the manager's made against her written assignments, and her boss can help reprioritize them, given the always changing needs of the business.

These sessions always start with the subordinate reading aloud the minutes of the previous meeting. This gives the meeting structure and organization. It's a natural follow-through from the last meeting. This reminds both parties of what was discussed at the last meeting, and provides a way to share what has been accomplished since then.

Typically, the first time a new employee experiences this process, one can read the surprise on his face. And then, after a puzzled pause, the person will frequently say, "You actually want me to read these aloud? I read them carefully when I wrote them last month."

"Yes," I'll reply. "I do want you to read them aloud."

This is detail, and it works! The minutes become an agenda. Reading the minutes almost always triggers considerable discussion and, often, major modification. Sometimes it leads to the reversal of a decision. Other times, it can lead to a deep discussion of execution issues.

Jim Fox, our deputy director of investments whom I introduced in Chapter Seven, had come to work for us with impressive credentials. Trained as an engineer, he was a summa cum laude graduate of Case Western Reserve's School of Engineering and had worked for General Electric for eight years. He had started his GE life as an engineer, later moving into product management. In the evenings, Jim earned his MBA at Case Western's Weatherhead School, where he was brought to my attention by professor Richard Osborne, who has been a friend of mine for years. Even coming from a company as disciplined and execution focused as GE, Jim confesses to being surprised by our precision. His thoughts:

I actually welcomed the chance to have a one-on-one opportunity with Mort. I went to his office for my first meeting and showed up with a blank sheet of paper. When he asked me to jot down the minutes of the session, there was no surprise on my part. I already had a three-week orientation at the company, and I was assigned a buddy who explained pretty much everything I needed to know about factbooks. So Mort and I have our first meeting together, and I write the minutes up later in the day, describing what I think happened. I got it back from Mort the next day with pencil marks on it. Mort essentially said, "This isn't what actually happened. Instead, this is what we agreed to do." It was a precision that was definitely eye opening. There was no room for confusion on the next steps.

Truth is, I was a little bit surprised because it's so rigorous for just a two-person meeting. At first, some people think it's strange. I've been on both sides of it because Mort not only does it with his direct reports but we, in turn, do it with our staff. The one thing that is without negotiation is that there are going to be formal minutes and assignments. Mort sees the minutes of the meetings with folks I have on my team. He'll even go through and edit the minutes of the meetings that he wasn't in. In a way, it's almost like changing history. For the most part, he'll say it looks good. But sometimes he might come back and say, "Whoa, how does this assignment fit into what we agreed to? Let's talk about this."

Now, when I have meetings with people, I want a recap immediately afterward. I've come to appreciate the value of how that insures that there are never misunderstandings. Everyone is rowing in the same direction. I haven't pulled out a three-ring binder with my five-year-old son, but it's not over yet.

Jim Fox might think he's joking, but I've actually had colleagues who used factbooks to organize their personal lives. In any case, once the minutes are read, we'll go to the more specific assignments and discuss some of them in detail. There's rarely a doubt in an employee's mind as to what she is supposed to do, and the priority for working on projects. Getting into this level of detail on each assignment also signals to employees that you care about what they do and how they do it.

Then we'll typically do deeper dives into some assignments. There will generally be a tab with additional documentation on certain active projects.

After the meeting, the employee is responsible for creating a set of minutes. These minutes are sent back to the supervisor as soon as possible. They are sometimes corrected by the boss as needed, and then placed into both three-ring binders for the next session.

The factbook system is a great way to stay on track and make real decisions, with built-in accountability. When a meeting is over, there is great clarity. Both parties know what to do. The face-to-face interaction also allows subordinates to push back when there is too much on their plate or if a project proves to be much harder than initially anticipated.

The benefits are clear:

1. The system can make you a better professional. A factbook helps you stay organized and disciplined. It enables you to always be working on the right things, as agreed every month with your boss.
2. The system ensures that the most important work gets done first, by putting a laser-like focus on an individual's work plan and carefully setting priorities.

3. The system makes you feel more engaged. You can't go through this process and not understand just what is expected of you. It reinforces our culture as well, reminding us that we must stay focused on what we do if we want to achieve superior execution.

One of the most difficult tasks any leader has is to get the full story from his subordinates. It's only natural for people to try to please the boss. So as a leader you're less likely to get the full truth unless you have a way to find it. These structured meetings help you discover what's getting done and what isn't. The planning my managers do with their subordinates will reflect the planning I do with them. Because I get the minutes of factbook meetings between my subordinates and their direct reports, I can see in detail what people are doing a layer down and how our goals and objectives cascade through the organization. This gives me a deeper understanding of what is actually happening on the ground.

After reading minutes, I'll sometimes call a manager and ask how a particular agenda item fits into our overall plan. I've often heard other CEOs say that they have very qualified people and that the CEO's job is to stay out of their way. That is not my style. I believe in working shoulder to shoulder with my subordinates. I believe I'm their "partner." I can't be a true partner to them if I don't know enough about what they do and how they do it. At the same time, the CEO's challenge is to permit creativity and encourage the team to openly disagree when they believe another solution might be better.

Factbooks create a way for people to deeply understand the policies and strategies that make for excellence in execution. Factbooks are the sheet music a leader needs to expertly play a symphony.

CHAPTER 9

Why We Swung Our Acquisitions Bat to Hit Singles, Not Home Runs

BUSINESS IS MAINLY ABOUT TAKING ADVANTAGE OF OPPORTUNITIES. By the mid-1960s, Premier had become a very successful company. In 1964, Premier reached another milestone when our company's shares were accepted for trading on the New York Stock Exchange. Every year, the company's earnings and revenues had shown significant growth.

By the mid-1960s, we knew we had to be in electronics. It was the wave of the future, and it clearly was an industry already booming. As mentioned earlier, we found a midsize distributor in Chicago called Newark Electronics through a business broker who represented the Poncher brothers, who owned the business. Sam Poncher was president; his brother Abe was executive vice president and head of purchasing. Both had been running the family company for thirty-five years. By then, it was already one of the largest electronic parts distributors in the country. We saw a lot of upside in extending their sales throughout North America. The Poncher family held about 40 percent of the company and wanted to sell out for cash.

After much haggling, we shook hands on a $22 million deal. We started talking at $18 million, so the negotiation had already brought the price up by $4 million. Jim Lynn, then our outside counsel, was helping us with the merger.

A day after the handshake, however, Lynn received a call from Newark's attorney, Ken Prince.

"Jim, I'm embarrassed to tell you this," Prince said. "I know we settled on the price yesterday, but my clients want $1 million more."

Lynn called to relay the news, and he was shocked and offended that a deal we both thought was done was still open to more negotiation.

It didn't take me too long to think about it. Even at $1 million more, I thought it was a good deal for us.

"Give it to them," I told him.

"All right; I'll call Ken and tell him we will do it."

The next day, I got another call from Lynn.

"You're not going to believe this," he said, "but they're not going to do the deal unless you give them still another million. Mort, they're raking you over the coals. Are you sure you want to do this?"

I told Lynn I needed another day to think about it. At the time, Newark was making about 3 percent after taxes, $1.06 million on $33.4 million in annual sales. Premier, which was generating 10 percent after tax, was then earning almost four times as much as Newark on roughly the same revenue. We ended our previous fiscal year with earnings of $3.87 million on sales of $35.3 million.

If we could get Newark to just half our level of profitability, we could easily double their income. At the very least, we figured it was good for $2.5 million a year, even if we couldn't increase

Newark's sales volume. Judging from what I saw during my walk-through of their facility, I suspected the company was underman-aged. We'd be able to bring discipline, order, and focus to this business, and that could make a very big difference in its earnings potential. I took a long view of it: What might this deal mean to us ten years from now? Under the best scenario, our business could explode. With that possibility in mind, paying another million was not hard. It's easy to get caught up in the excitement of the chase and then to overpay. But this was a bet on the future—not the present.

We completed the deal on November 27, 1968—six months after we publicly said we were in negotiations to buy Newark—and it became the most successful of the twelve acquisitions we made at Premier. Newark became the growth engine for our company. It was the most explosive acquisition we made. It changed the company so that more than 60 percent of our revenue would be in electronics. Years later, it would be the major reason why Farnell Electronics in the United Kingdom agreed to pay nearly $3 billion to merge with Premier in 1996.

The lesson? If you buy something of value, such as a painting by an established artist, or even a business, it's okay to overpay a little if what you might get out of it is a lot. It can be much more painful to let it get away from you. This is especially true when you are trying to buy something of value from an owner who has been emotionally involved in the business. That owner has to feel that he or she is getting a good price to let go of the prize. Yet if the Ponchers had come back for still more money, we may well have not done the deal.

To summarize, Newark met our criteria for a deal:

First and foremost, we looked for distribution businesses with strong market positions—as opposed to superior technology or manufacturing prowess or laboratory skills. Having a solid foothold in a market was important to us because the Premier leadership team was stacked with sales and marketing types. So a company with a strong market position played to our strengths. If I were running a company whose success was based on technology, I'd be scouring the market for acquisitions that built on our existing technology so as to extend and strengthen our current market position.

Second, we looked for businesses that were undermanaged. It's why I felt so strongly that a few million more for Newark didn't make that big a difference. I believed we could bring our management discipline and systems to the company to improve its profitability. That was true of our very first acquisition, Akron Brass, in 1962. This company, which makes firefighting equipment, was one of two leaders in the field when we bought it. It was a bit sleepy, too, which meant that by giving it a bit of love and attention, we could improve the profit margins of the operation, which we did.

Undermanaged companies appeal to me. If you can improve the operations of an organization that has been poorly managed, you know you can make a difference. It's the path toward taking an ordinary business and turning it into something extraordinary. We've been able to do that, time and time again. Few companies have the structured, organized systems that ensure quality execution. The potential upside there creates considerable confidence that the right buyer can get more out of the company, its people, its customers, and its products. That's why undermanaged companies offer big opportunities for disciplined management.

Undermanaged companies are rarely fanatics about customer service. We were. If we could provide Newark's customers with service they had never seen before, we would be able to charge fair prices. If you "kill yourself for your customer," they will pay you sufficiently for the product. By then, we had proved to ourselves that superior customer service could bring huge advantages. It would be true at Newark and at most of the other companies we acquired.

Third, we bought niches, not size. With the exception of Newark, which doubled our revenue in a single deal, we mostly swung the acquisition bat to hit singles, not home runs. Singles hitters strike out less in baseball and in business. Solidly hit singles through the infield will do just fine. It wasn't about hitting tape-measure home runs. Instead, we took only carefully calculated risks and never made a bet-the-company gamble. Why? People some-times do outsized deals in the service of their own egos or to placate Wall Street analysts. Many CEOs go for the big bet because it fits their image of themselves and is what's expected of them. We always saw our job as increasing shareholder value, not building our personal image.

There's hardly ever a good reason to overreach. Too few mergers ever work out to their full potential. We started plenty of new things and acquired a good number of companies. But the risks were always manageable. I think we're proof that you can grow a business in a way that minimizes risk.

Fourth, patience and understanding are crucial to getting a good deal. I remember the time we were keen on acquiring a company called D-A Lubricant, a maker of industrial lubricants. I first talked to the CEO, Tom Binford, in 1961, and he had no interest in a merger. I approached him again two years later, and he had changed his mind. We had dinner together at a downtown hotel in Cleveland in 1963 and shook hands on a deal. The next morning, my phone rang. It was Binford.

"Mort," he said, "I just can't do it." I understood his emotional attachment to a business his father had founded, and I moved on. Several more years went by until we got together again in 1967.

"This time, I'm finally ready," he told me. He went back to his home and business in Indianapolis. I didn't get a phone call the next morning, so I felt pretty confident we had a deal. But the following day, I received a letter from him. It was another "Dear Mort: I just can't do it." We got together a third time in 1969, a full eight years from my first overture, and finally did the deal. It was the eighth division we acquired in the 1960s.

Fifth, sometimes what you don't do is more important than what you do. One thing we tended not to do was to try to consolidate a business segment by acquiring bolt-on companies in the same business. The basic reason was culture. Putting competitors in the same business together is fraught with problems that can take years to overcome. If you buy a company that already has a strong market position, you should be able to grow the business from that solid base.

We pretty much stuck to our knitting when we bought something: we sought companies in the industrial market, not the consumer market, and companies that sell products used for maintenance and repair. By eliminating consumer companies and those that make original equipment rather than replacement parts, we were able to narrow the field in a way that increased our likelihood of success.

Finally, the most important part of making a deal successful is culture. Many mergers and acquisitions never realize their full potential because the cultures of the two companies fail to mesh. One company tends to suffocate the other. What's often lost or sacrificed are the things that made the acquired company special or unique. That is why we rarely moved quickly to change people. Once we bought a company, we tried to learn everything we could about the people who worked there. We didn't want to cut the brains and heart out of the company. Instead, we spent months getting to know the top people. We would identify the A's, B's, and C's during that time, and we would create a plan to keep the A's, move around the B's, and get the C's out. You can't do this overnight. It takes time and patience to get it right. Too often, a CEO wants to prove that an acquisition shows immediate benefits and will immediately cut costs. Often he will reduce the most important assets—the people—first. This can be a serious mistake. It often is.

It all comes back to the home run analogy. When you are trying to hit a single, you're not overswinging or overreaching. And when you are taking the necessary time to know the human assets you've acquired in a deal, you're not looking to make a big immediate write-off to impress Wall Street. Instead, you're showing the kind of disciplined patience at the plate that will increase the chance that you'll get a hit.

Trying for home runs can work. Going for singles works better.

CHAPTER 10

Lighting Candles

ON AN EVENING IN THE SPRING OF 1954, I chaired my first meeting of a nonprofit organization. I was in my early thirties, had been active in the United Way since age twenty-six, and was now beginning my first leadership role. I had just taken over the chairmanship of the small business division of United Way from a lawyer, someone I admired, George Baldwin. Our role was to raise money for the charity from smaller businesses in the Cleveland metro area.

I asked George to come to the first meeting I chaired at the Statler Hotel in Cleveland, in order to critique my chairmanship. After chairing that first session, I felt good. We had a very constructive meeting and what I thought was a great exchange of ideas. My friend George saw it differently.

"Mort, it was a very creative meeting," he said. "There were some wonderful decisions and some great conclusions for United Way. But you know it would have been a lot better if those people left the meeting thinking it was their meeting instead of your meeting. Practically all of the ideas were yours."

His observation hit me like a ton of bricks. I realized that I had thoroughly dominated the meeting and not been aware of it. George's honesty changed me. In that moment, I learned what would become important to my ability to lead: to allow a group to come up with and help shape the ideas, not to personally dominate. If people feel ownership, there will be a better result. Involvement leads to understanding, and understanding leads to commitment. When everyone is given a chance to engage and participate, the result is inevitably improved. Working together, you end up with a stronger, better result than you could ever achieve on your own. That was a transformative leadership experience for me.

What made the lesson even more powerful was that it did not occur in a business setting, but rather in a world that became every bit as important to me as my business career—the social sector. Over these years I have picked up all kinds of lessons and ideas from my nonprofit experience, often learning from observing the behavior of other business executives on various nonprofit boards. The leadership lessons I gained in this way were far more important than I could have predicted.

On reflection, I'm betting that if I had been born into a middle-class family, I would have been a social worker. I think of the world as having a huge number of candles, and only a small percentage are lit. I know now that I have devoted a big part of my life to lighting as many candles as I can. To light a candle is to make the world a better place. It's an uphill fight. It is a tough road because we will always be climbing. No doubt, we will never reach perfection.

My deep interest in the social sector can be traced directly to my mother. As the matriarch of our home, she had very few dollars and had to manage those dollars efficiently. Yet eight or nine times a year, someone would knock on the door and ask her for help. Sometimes a daughter was getting married and needed a dress. Other times, the fridge broke down and needed repair or replacing. Every time my mother would help someone in need, she would have the same simple answer to those she assisted: "Take it. You don't have to pay me back. You'll do something for me some day and we'll come out even." The money she gave up was perhaps for a new dress or pair of shoes she didn't buy for herself. Over the years, my brothers and I internalized that generosity. We inhaled it.

To me, all these years working in the social sector have been like living a dream. I share the dream of so many—to leave the world a better place, to do whatever one can to improve the lives of others who aren't as fortunate. What I also discovered is that living a life of meaning is one of the greatest gifts you can give to yourself. It's a way to achieve major fulfillment. Further, throughout my career, I learned perhaps as much about leadership working in the nonprofit world as I did in the world of business. This has been a major development opportunity for me.

That was true because of my early involvement in the social sector. I started almost literally from the ground up in 1946, soliciting small donations from small businesses in Cleveland for the United Way. I was all of twenty-five years old when I would call prospects and tell them that I had the pleasure and the privilege of soliciting their gift to the United Way.

"When would be the best time to visit you?" I'd ask.

There would often be a pause on the line. Once, I heard the person on the other end blurt out, "How about never!"

I would tell myself *I've got to get this guy*. I'd keep calling until I got on his calendar. And when I showed up, I'd explain that I was a volunteer and that my brothers and I had already given a gift, and I would explain why I felt passionately about the cause.

I learned that the more enthusiasm I showed and the more deeply I demonstrated my conviction for the cause, the more likely it was that I'd leave with a significant gift. I have been soliciting for the United Way and other causes every year since 1946.

I moved up the ranks to head various committees of the United Way of Cleveland, until I became president. So when I was invited to join the national board of the United Way, I generally knew how their process worked and sometimes how it could be run more effectively.

In 1953, my brothers and I formed a foundation because we felt that this would permit us a more efficient way to give our money away. I don't call that commitment of ours simply generosity. I think of it also as an obligation that goes beyond writing a check. And those feelings come from Rose Mandel, my mother.

In my career in the social sector, I have been personally or jointly responsible for initiating more than a dozen nonprofit organizations, from the Mandel Center for Non-Profit Organizations at Case Western Reserve University to the World Confederation for Jewish Community Centers, based in Jerusalem. Every once in a while, I was able to find a need in the landscape of social service, and often I tried to fill it.

The nonprofit world is where we spend much of our lives—in churches and synagogues, schools and hospitals, sports and the community. It is a world filled with potential and great opportunity, and far too much of it is unrealized.

Further, I believe that running either the United Way, a very successful nonprofit organization, or IBM, a very successful for-profit organization, is almost exactly the same process, except in the measurement of outcomes. What they both share in common is great leadership, strong core values, and disciplined execution.

One problem with nonprofits is that some leaders spend too much time talking about and defining their cause—and not enough time on addressing the management issues that might ultimately enable them to better help the people they are trying to serve.

A few years ago, McKinsey & Co.'s Institute for the Non-Profit Sector found that nonprofits could free up $100 billion each year simply by becoming more efficient and productive. The study, with former New Jersey senator Bill Bradley as its lead adviser, said that $55 billion of that money would materialize if the less-efficient organizations were as productive as the more cost-efficient ones. Never before had the opportunity to unleash massive cost savings been made so clear.

Three principles in the corporate world—respect for the individual, superior customer service, and the pursuit of excellence—are core values that can deliver as much impact in the social world. These ideas work in all settings. They apply to all firms that serve people, whether they are universities, hospitals, charitable organizations, or multinational corporations. They are the essence of great leadership.

For almost every nonprofit, there will always be too few dollars; the needs are so great. What we need to do is not only maximize the use of those dollars but also constantly raise the level of leadership so as to maximize the impact of our nonprofit institutions on society. There's nothing wrong with improving fundraising, but even more important is to find leadership talent able to produce effective change. We too often lessen the outcomes of our nonprofits through the inadequacy of the professional leadership. Another problem is that even though there are often good people on the job, not enough time or money is invested to give them the skills they need to be successful.

In my business career, I was extremely fortunate to have management thinker Peter Drucker as a mentor. In social causes, I was fortunate to have as a mentor an exceptional social worker named Henry Zucker. I met him in 1946 when he became associate director of Cleveland's Jewish Community Federation, which he would later head for some twenty-seven years. As an educator and a Jewish communal pathfinder, Henry was both a humble servant and an inspirational leader.

Henry was blessed with a remarkably creative and fertile mind, and he was always cooking up ideas. One time we shared a train ride from New York to Cleveland. The train was stalled by a snowstorm near Buffalo for an extra eight hours. Henry and I made worthwhile use of the time. By the time the train pulled into Cleveland, we had worked out the framework for a new organization to gain deeper engagement from foundations supporting the Jewish Community Federation. After Henry retired in 1976, I brought him into the Mandel Foundation as our executive director and mentor, and he stayed with us for seventeen years. During that time, Henry played a pivotal role in our largest single initiative: professional leadership development for the nonprofit sector.

Like me, Henry believed in the power of an individual to make a huge difference. Whether in the for-profit or nonprofit sector, it is all about having the most talented and capable people in key leadership roles. Often, the best ideas lose their power because of ineffective execution.

Over the years we worked together, he helped me light many candles. The one that burns brightest is our Mandel Foundation in Israel. In 1979, I had become a board member of the Jewish Agency of Israel, one of the most important Jewish organizations that serves as a link between Israel and Jewish communities all over the world. This was a post I held for eight years. It was through this association that I developed a very close working relationship with Seymour Fox, an American professor who had taught at the University of Chicago and Ohio State University and was the national head of Ramah Camps, and then later immigrated to Israel.

As the then dean of the School of Education at Hebrew University, Seymour was all these things: charismatic, brilliant, creative, and passionate. I had initially met him while he served as government representative to the Jewish Agency Foundation, which I chaired. After I came to know him better, I invited him to help us develop our committee process and program. Seymour turned out to be far more than a consulting adviser. He was an entrepreneur and a visionary who attracted exceptional people to our cause. We shared a vision to change the world by investing in superior people.

Seymour was well known and widely respected in the field of Jewish education. Recalls Rabbi David Ellenson, a longtime friend who is president of the Hebrew Union College in New York:

> You couldn't meet Seymour and not be impressed by his vast knowledge in philosophy, education, and classical Judaism. He was indefatigable, much like Mort. They were both intelligent, highly motivated, high-energy people with an infinite love for the Jewish people. Seymour was very impressive. You could not escape his intelligence when you were in his presence. Mort told me the story of one experience that sold him on Seymour shortly after Seymour was assigned to him. Before the first meeting of a national Commission on Jewish Education, which Mort was to chair, Mort came into the meeting room early to make sure everything was set up right. Seymour already had beaten him to the punch. He was there reviewing every detail.

Then, in 1988, after a meeting in Jerusalem of a new Jewish Agency committee on Jewish Education, which I chaired, Seymour and I found ourselves walking back to the King David Hotel, deeply engaged in discussing what we might be able to do on our own. We stood in front of the hotel and there decided to create a foundation office headquartered in Jerusalem to seek ways to train the next generation of Jewish education leaders.

"Let's build an IBM," I said, "an institution that could be one of the best in the world for our cause."

At the time, we were deeply concerned about the fact that large numbers of Jews in North America were losing interest in Jewish values, ideals, and behavior. The holocaust generation that celebrated the formation of Israel profoundly felt its Jewish heritage and responsibility. But as anti-Semitism began to diminish, some of the sons and daughters of that earlier generation increasingly came to believe that Judaism had a lesser role to play in their search for personal fulfillment and sense of community. Intermarriage between Jews and non-Jews had risen dramatically, and a significant proportion of children from those marriages no longer identified themselves as active Jews.

Yet most Jewish leaders were focused on other important issues: helping Israel become a more viable country, strengthening their own local Jewish community, the continuing repair of Jewish life in highly distressed countries, and assisting the emigration of Russian Jews to Israel. I believed that Jewish continuity could best be served by strengthening Jewish education. There was already an extensive system of education for Jews in North America in school classrooms, community centers, summer camps, and educational trips to Israel. But they were often underfunded and underused, and there were deficiencies in what was taught.

In 1988, our foundation recruited a stellar cast of leading Jewish educators, religious leaders, and successful entrepreneurs from both the for-profit and nonprofit worlds to a special commission to study this issue and then to develop a blueprint for action. The Commission on Jewish Education in North America brought together dramatically different viewpoints on Jewish life, including the heads of the three major Jewish seminaries representing the reform, the conservative, and the Orthodox movements of the Jewish faith.

After two years of meetings and deliberation, the outcome of this effort was a landmark report, "A Time to Act," which was published in late 1990. Among other things, the commission urged the building of a serious profession of Jewish education to get the best and brightest people into that field. It called on top community leaders to support the cause of Jewish education and to raise the issue to the top of the communal agenda. It also led to the creation of the Council for Initiatives in Jewish Education, aimed at driving the changes necessary to make a difference.

In the years that followed, there have been vast and profound improvements in Jewish education in the United States and Canada. New day schools have opened and flourished along with strengthened congregational Hebrew schools, and more Jews have been able to connect with Jewish values and ideals through the expansion and growth of Jewish Community Centers across America.

This experience deepened my willingness to invest even more heavily in seeking a stronger Jewish future. So, in 1990, we began our journey to focus on Jewish education with the creation of the Mandel Foundation in Jerusalem. We had an official opening ceremony attended by Israeli educators and senior government officials. Among those present at the dedication was the minister of education, Zevulun Hammer.

Annette Hochstein, an educational consultant who worked closely with us on the commission report and later succeeded

Seymour as president of the Mandel Foundation-Israel, recalls an early part of the story:

> In December of 1990, shortly after the Jerusalem office of the Mandel Foundation opened and several weeks after we finished the report of the Commission on Jewish Education in North America, Seymour and Mort responded to a request from Minister Zevulun Hammer to meet with him. They met for dinner in a Chinese restaurant in Tel Aviv. Mort, who knew and admired the minister, got up from the table when he came into the restaurant, and they hugged.
>
> "Mort," Hammer said, "you do very good things. This is my third term as Minister of Education, and I have a terrible shortage of policy-level people in my department to run the country's K–12 education system. Can you help me? You know how to train leaders." Mort told him, "We don't do this kind of training, but we will think seriously about your request." As they drove home from that meeting, both Mort and Seymour had a feeling that possibly history was being made.

After a planning group made up of ministry and foundation representatives had met for about a year, we were able to launch the Mandel School for Educational Leadership (MSEL), funded one-third by the government and two-thirds by the Mandel Foundation and other private sector partners. The noble mission of this effort was to turn out exemplary leaders in education, the kind of people who inspire greatness in others, who can accomplish the extraordinary. The biggest bet of all is the bet on people. If we could train and develop people capable of helping build a striving society, we would certainly succeed in lighting more candles.

So we imagined and decided to build over time a world-class staff that would train high-potential people to be effective leaders, from social entrepreneurs in the education sector to school principals and Ministry of Education officials. The institute was grounded in the values of pluralism, respecting the ambition of the Israeli government to significantly improve K–12 education.

We created a program to train leaders for K–12 general education in Israel. This was a challenging two-year program that recruited already successful professionals, often with master's degrees or PhDs, to train them to become effective leaders in the field of general education. Everyone who attended this school would find his or her beliefs and attitudes shaken to the ground. Today, the program's success has established the MSEL as a highly successful institution—one that has become widely admired and respected. Some of the leading scholars who teach at Mandel have turned down invitations to teach at such major universities as Oxford and Harvard so they that can remain at MSEL.

What the MSEL has helped create is a corps of change agents, more than four hundred graduates who are transforming Israel through ideas and action that improve the lives of Israelis. Together, our graduates represent a virtual who's who of Israeli education and society. Some are leading progressive schools that bring together Jews and Arabs in classrooms where children are taught tolerance and acceptance. Others are educating the next generation of Israel's leadership, future prime ministers and Nobel Prize winners. And they are helping the country chart its future course.

Every day, they pay tribute to what I so profoundly believe: that a single individual can change the world. Powerful ideas, driven by outstanding people, represent a sure way to light more candles and help illuminate the world.

CHAPTER 11

A Gospel of Wealth

(With Apologies to Andrew Carnegie)

IN THE LATE 1880s, the great philanthropist Andrew Carnegie made the case that wealthy capitalists had a responsibility to play a broader cultural and social role in life. In short, they were duty bound to improve the world with their wealth. But in his well-publicized essay "Wealth," Carnegie warned that there was peril in handing out large sums of money to people or organizations that were ill equipped to make the best use of those gifts. The industrialist argued that wealthy entrepreneurs must assume the responsibility of distributing their fortunes in a way that increased the odds that the money would be put to good and effective use.

I've given much thought to Carnegie's philanthropic principles. Over the years, I've come up with my own views on how to efficiently give money away—and in many cases I agree with Carnegie that the responsibility falls on the giver of money to ensure that it is used smartly and effectively.

At the Mandel Foundation, we have evolved a few operating principles that have come to define my own philanthropic philosophy:

115

One principle will not surprise any reader of this book: We believe in and bet on people, striving to have the best possible people on our board and staff. Our standards are high. We are determined to recruit, motivate, and retain exceptional people. What we accomplish will be the result of having board members and staffers who are smart, thoughtful, passionate, committed, and caring.

Second, our philanthropy is pursued as systematically as our business interests. We create mission statements, clear goals, and formal work plans to achieve our objectives. We engage in continuous review. In our pursuit of excellence, we tend to stay somewhat dissatisfied, always trying to raise the bar. We constantly ask ourselves whether, in the words of John Gardner, we are maintaining our sense of direction or just leaping at a "wonderful opportunity" that may, in fact, be a diversion of our time and money.

We invest more and more of our time and money in research and evaluation, in collecting data, and in trying to be as informed as possible when we make decisions. Like other philanthropic organizations, we've struggled to measure our success and to monitor and evaluate our investments.

Third, in keeping with Carnegie's philosophy that a giver of money must assume responsibility for the "good and effective use" of his fortune, I also believe, as the foundation CEO, that I am fully responsible. It's hard work to give money away thoughtfully. I'm deeply passionate about that. I want to entrust our philanthropy to a board and staff I genuinely believe will be strong advocates and believers of the causes in which we invest. I did not come to these conclusions without much thought. In fact, back in March of 1999, Lee Shulman, a longtime friend and adviser to our foundation who was then president of the Carnegie Foundation for the Advancement of Teaching, had organized a private conference for me at Stanford University with John Gardner and the heads of some of the largest and most influential philanthropic foundations in the country—Rockefeller, Carnegie, Hewlett, and others. It was a glorious two-day event in which we discussed how best to ensure the continuity of the Mandel Foundation. A good deal of the conversation centered on when and whether I should entrust our philanthropy to a chief executive who would then report to a board on which I would sit as chairman.

I was especially honored to be in the same room with Gardner, who had been secretary of health, education and welfare in the 1960s and a former president of the Carnegie Corporation. He had founded two influential nonprofit organizations in his lifetime: Common Cause and Independent Sector. At the time, he was eighty-six years old and as wise as an owl.

We had spent most of one afternoon discussing how some of the oldest and most influential foundations in the United States had managed to remain alive, fresh, and vital when their founders were all long gone. They largely did so by recruiting highly committed trustees to their boards who installed highly professional chief executives. But there was always a question of timing: when should the founder step aside in favor of a nonfamily successor?

For most of my adult life, I had felt tremendous fulfillment simultaneously leading both a business and a philanthropic enterprise.

Then, at one point, Gardner turned to me and said, with great conviction, that I should not turn over a role that brings me profound satisfaction.

"You know, Mort," he said, "it strikes me that this is something that means a great deal to you. My instinct would be to write down a general succession plan that you revise periodically. And for you to maintain your own involvement until you conclude that you don't want to. Because it seems to me that it would be an extraordinarily painful and difficult thing for you to give this organization to someone to run while you were in good form. At this stage in your life, there is no real need to hand over an institution, which embodies the most fundamental elements of your soul, to somebody else. You will know at some point when you are ready."

So for these many years, I have remained the chairman and chief executive of the Mandel Foundation. I have held myself accountable for the success or failure of our philanthropic investments because this has been, as Gardner put it so well, "a fundamental element" of my soul.

• • •

Here are the big ideas that define our giving:

1. By and large, we are drawn to tough, persistent problems that aren't easily solved. So my brothers and I have focused much of our giving on challenges that require long-term commitment. Leadership, education, managing nonprofit organizations, urban development, and Jewish education are issues that are stubbornly persistent. They can be ameliorated, but it would be hard to ever declare victory over these challenges and walk away.

Philanthropy is likely to have a longer attention span—often more than government—in solving certain intractable problems. So it makes sense for philanthropy to address issues that justify long-term commitments.

2. In recent years, venture philanthropy has become quite popular. The idea is similar to the use of venture capital to help entrepreneurs create businesses. But social problems are not business opportunities. Once you invest in a social cause, it rarely will generate cash—as a business does—that would allow an institution to eventually become self-sustaining.

That's why we sometimes make grants that are open ended. It's a commitment to support a cause or issue over a number of years—but not forever. Such grants are not a blank check. An organization that receives a multiyear grant is required to report on its progress on a regular basis, so we have some notion of whether the dollars are being spent wisely. There are scheduled meetings and operating reviews that allow us to monitor progress.

3. In all of our endeavors, we seek to attract and involve people with great personal integrity, people who show deep commitment to a high standard of morality and ethics. Throughout our leadership training programs, we stress the importance of values in shaping effective leaders. Positive values are a necessary condition for top leadership.

4. In recent years we have placed a good deal of effort into seeking ways to strengthen and invigorate the study of humanities. At the Mandel Leadership Institute in Israel, fellows spend a great deal of time on ethics and philosophy. The courses they take address the big questions: What is a life worth living? What constitutes a good society? We are the beneficiaries of centuries of wisdom developed by countless thinkers, scholars, and scientists. We stand on the shoulders of Confucius, Socrates, Aristotle, Maimonides, al-Farabi, Shakespeare, Voltaire, and many, many others. Their powerful ideas should be studied by each new generation.

Among our recent grants are a newly opened building devoted to the humanities at Brandeis University in Boston, and we have made still a second major grant for a new humanities building and program at Hebrew University in Jerusalem.

The humanities are the embodiment, the essence of the human spirit.

Yet the humanities are today the road less traveled within the circles of higher education. Their role in education has been challenged in recent years as they have been overshadowed by more pragmatic domains, such as law, medicine, business, and the sciences. Funding for the humanities has lagged in the face of such factors as skyrocketing college costs, reduced emphasis on the teaching of humanities in high schools, and serious job placement concerns.

The humanities are unlike medicine, business, or technology— one doesn't engage in them for the sake of some immediate utility. One engages in them because they bring us closer to what is basic and beautiful and sublime about the world.

• • •

So these big ideas define our giving. I think Andrew Carnegie would be pleased.

CHAPTER 12

Using Business Ideas in the Social Sector

HOW DO YOU BRING EVER-BETTER PLANNING AND EVER-BETTER EXECUTION TO THE SOCIAL SECTOR?

I believe that the same core ideas that have helped make me—and countless others—successful in the for-profit world have helped make me more effective in the world of social service.

As Peter Drucker once said, the social sector needs management and discipline as much as—perhaps even more than—business does, precisely because nonprofits lack the discipline of the bottom line. Knowing client needs is not a substitute for (1) strong executive leadership, (2) an unrelenting focus on staffing with great people, (3) a culture that is both client and staff oriented, and (4) a commitment to excellent execution, all of which produce superior service for your clients.

These ideas flow both ways. Business hardly has a monopoly on management principles that lead to efficiency, innovation, and renewal. There are brilliantly led nonprofit enterprises that can teach many business leaders a thing or two. For many nonprofits, powerful and dramatic results can come from seemingly simple tools and techniques commonly used in business. The transfer of these ideas can be a tipping point for social service, a way to increase the good that comes from each donated dollar, a way to touch perhaps millions of additional lives.

Let me give you one example: benchmarking. The idea of looking for organizations that do some things exceptionally well and then studying those "best practices" so that you learn from them is a basic idea in the business world. It can also be a lever for positive change in the social world.

For seven years now, the Mandel Foundation has been funding a comprehensive benchmarking program for Jewish Community Centers (JCCs). In any given year, more than thirty JCCs in North America agree to participate in an ongoing study that examines more than two dozen factors critical to success, from financial sustainability and user engagement to program performance and staff motivation.

Everyone is rarely best at everything. But by finding who is best at what, the underperformers have significantly benefited from the lessons of the best performers. Just knowing that other organizations can do something better than your own can shake a leadership team out of complacency. Often, as the CEOs of centers learn more about their operations, they are able to stretch their dollars and do more for their members.

At the 150 JCCs in the United States, there are hundreds of thousands of members. Given that the JCCs want to retain those members and also gain greater financial support from them, there are some obvious things a center can do. Our benchmarking studies revealed one not-so-obvious practice by closely studying the centers most successful at retention and donor support. They found that if JCC staff regularly engaged in brief, informal conversations with visiting members, those members were more likely to renew their membership and far more likely to offer additional financial help to the center.

Surprisingly, this all came down to whether a staff person greeted a member by name and engaged in "small talk." Simply remembering a detail about the member's life, showing some interest and concern for that member, proved to make a dramatic difference in members' satisfaction.

The numbers that come from a sophisticated analysis make the case: more JCC members were "very likely" to support the center financially if they had informal conversations with staff more than three out of every four visits; but if they were greeted this way less than half the time, fewer than half were "very likely" to contribute financially. Small talk apparently has big potential.

Also, a smile makes a huge difference. We knew that friendliness was good, but we didn't know it was hugely good. Many JCCs have put small talk in place with measurable results. It was clear that a concerted effort should be made to encourage staff to make user engagement a priority. With such convincing data in hand, leaders are now able to make the necessary changes to help build and strengthen their organizations. Adopting a best practice is good business. Everybody wins.

Todd Rockoff, the executive director of the JCC in Akron, Ohio, has seen and acted on the power of this benchmarking analysis:

> Three years ago, we had a very large desk right in the middle of our fitness center. Staff would sit behind it and answer questions. After we read the benchmarking study, we literally ripped the desk out. It was four feet high. Taking it away proved the point. The whole mood changed in the room. Yet it was not that evident to us that this desk was such a physical and mental barrier to members.

Managing with this information has really changed the game for me and many of my colleagues. Benchmarking energizes people because you know that it can help you to identify a jewel of an opportunity to improve. The goal is to run your core business as effectively as you can, and benchmarking makes a big difference.

Last year, we discovered that our early childhood department was performing at well below the average financial surplus for a JCC of our size. We asked those centers that did it better what they were doing to improve their performance and resulting financial success. We identified some things we needed to do: change our class sizes and also the number of classes we offered. Today, we're doing much better, and it's because my team used the benchmarking data that enabled us to tap the knowledge of our colleagues.

Just this one move has helped us improve financial results by a quarter of a million dollars. Benchmarking has allowed us to identify what our core businesses are, and how to make better decisions. Only a few years ago, there was no such comparative data. Now we are able to look at our member retention rate and how it compares with others. Now we use hard data as our guide to better decision making in all of our efforts.

Clearly, by taking the JCCs apart in terms of forty elements of their practices, we have helped centers, even those at the top of their game, find specific ways to improve.

Some centers stimulate staff creativity by holding contests to reward employees who learn the most member names. Other centers rotate staff—including senior executives—to serve as "greeters" at the front door. These are big, actionable insights that would never have been discovered if not for using this benchmarking tool.

The most basic of all principles is getting the very best people—the A players—in the key leadership jobs of an organization. This takes a concerted effort at human resource development. The goal:

to have every job filled by someone who is highly qualified. To do that, the key factors for success need to be well defined to help understand what kind of people are needed for these jobs. So, what are the attributes that make it more likely that a person will succeed in a position?

Nothing is more vital to the performance of an organization than the system by which people are nurtured and moved into positions where they can make their best contribution. A commitment to the continuing development of the professional staff is what management development is all about: ensuring that a person's full promise has a chance to be realized.

If you have a large enough organization, you may have a staff position—someone who helps the CEO manage this function. In smaller organizations, a consultant can help match the skills and attributes of each staff member with the desired outcomes. It's not uncommon to find plenty of mismatches on an existing team. The inventory of key leadership skills can guide both future recruitment as well as personal development.

Several years ago, we decided to create and fund the Mandel Center for Leadership Excellence within the Jewish Federations of North America (JFNA), the umbrella organization for 157 local federations. Each federation is both local and autonomous. It has a professional staff and a volunteer board of trustees. Each federation pays dues to the national organization and receives various services in return. Our plan in funding this center was simple: How do we increase the number of A-quality professional leaders who staff Jewish federations?

To lead this effort, JFNA brought in Deborah Smith, a consultant with rich human resource development experience. Debbie had worked with Xerox, Merck, Bausch & Lomb, and Coty. Currently, alongside other HR units now under her leadership, she runs a four-person search department. Those search consultants seek A players for important leadership jobs at federations.

It is Debbie's job to persuade federations to fully use her HR services. I'll let her explain it:

> Everything we do is guided by the belief that people make the difference. I once met Peter Drucker while I worked for Xerox and remember two things that he said: (1) "Stop focusing on what is wrong. Focus on what is right and do more of it." And (2) "You say more about your values and who you are by the people you hire than in all of the speeches you'll ever give."
>
> So the first part of my job is helping local Jewish federations to recruit and select the best possible people. If we can get more A's in the top jobs, it's the best way to improve the entire organization.
>
> The second part of my job is training and developing the people we already have. Our job is to convince federation leadership, professional and volunteer, to seek and keep the best. That's the only way to get superior performance.

Debbie is bringing discipline and planning to the human asset side of these organizations. She's helping make "the people part" of the business a conscious part of managing in a nonprofit environment.

• • •

Accomplished organizations are living, changing entities that require our full commitment. Each of us every day subconsciously decides to commit to renewal and growth or static and decay. There is great opportunity in bringing managerial practices used in business to the nonprofit sector—such as disciplined planning and a focus on A players. In the for-profit sector, we made money because often our competitors lacked the discipline to be efficient and productive. We can summon organizations to greatness by bringing disciplined management into their mind-set. It's an insistence on hiring the best people, building a strong culture, offering superior client satisfaction, living by well-established values, and ensuring superior execution.

Whether you are leading a for-profit company or a social enterprise, in the end, it's the soft stuff that can bring about hard results and major impact.

CHAPTER 13

An Olive Tree

ONE OF THE MOST TOUCHING MOMENTS OF MY BUSINESS LIFE
OCCURRED IN EARLY 2010 IN A SMALL TOWN IN SOUTHERN ISRAEL.
Little more than five years earlier, we had purchased Phoenicia
Glass Works Ltd., a glass plant that made bottles in Yerucham, a
small town in the Negev, a less developed part of Israel. That day,
on one of my regular visits, the Phoenicia CEO, Amnon Cohen,
told me that some of the plant's workers wanted to see me in the
garden. I was puzzled by the request.

After lunch, I went to the garden, where about fifty employees
had gathered. It was a clear and sunny day, beautiful in every way.
There, the three union leaders themselves had planted a young
olive tree in my honor along with a very artistic metal plaque that
read, "In Appreciation to Mort Mandel, A Great Employer." It was
a stunning moment, made even more meaningful when I learned
that the union itself had paid for the tree and the plaque and also
for a menorah, crafted by the same artist, for me to bring home
as a memento of this event.

The union steward gave a heartfelt speech in Hebrew that was
filled with appreciation and thanks for the much improved work

environment we had created, and for the prospect of a stronger future for the workers. As the words were translated for me, I had a hard time holding it together. Next to the union steward were other union leaders. What was on their faces? Respect and admiration.

The treatment I would normally have expected was courtesy. However, in this case, I also felt their affection and gratitude. They could have just said the words to me, but they wanted something "living" that would be present and visible for many years. For me, it was an overwhelming experience without parallel in my business career. I thanked all of them profusely. It was a moment I will carry with me forever.

Phoenicia is a living case study of meeting the expectations of workers, customers, shareholders, and the larger community in which the company exists. It is proof that it's possible to balance profit motives with corporate social responsibility without sacrificing either. And it represents textbook execution, by a carefully recruited and highly motivated management team, of the ideas and principles I've developed over a lifetime.

I thought back to the first time I had seen the property in 2004. The tall gates I went through were not at all welcoming. The grounds were barren, with no grass or trees. We later found out that some of the inventory on hand was of poor quality, and we decided much of it should not be sold.

During my first tour of the plant after we acquired the company, I had noticed that the workers avoided eye contact. There were no smiles. The faces were expressionless. Obviously, promises to these people had been broken—and on many occasions.

During this same tour, I told the existing chief executive that I needed to use the restroom. He offered his office bathroom, but instead I went into the nearest plant employee restroom. It was messy. To me, that was a telltale sign of the indifference that management felt for its employees. It was clear to me that this management didn't place a high enough value on the work environment.

The company was losing money. It had had three different owners in the previous five years. The number of defects in the company's output was unacceptably high. So was the employee accident rate.

Moshe Weksler, who was CEO of Israel Equity Ltd., our corporate headquarters unit based in Tel Aviv, and who led the effort to purchase Phoenicia Glass Works, tells the story well:

> It was a mess. In the preceding four years, the company had lost more than $40 million. There were no senior managers with the exception of the CEO. The plant equipment was old, and there was no serious inspection of the bottles. The company was always on the edge, and as a result they kept squeezing the workers.
>
> No one listened to the people working the machinery about how to improve the plant. These were people with as much as forty years of experience in this plant.
>
> However, Mort saw the potential. He knew we could improve the business, so it wasn't hard for him to buy the place. After doing careful due diligence, we bought it. Later, some businesspeople I know called and asked me, "Why in the world would you buy Phoenicia? It's a mess."

The answer was that we saw a great opportunity. Despite the problems, and even with quality issues that forced the company to recycle a high percentage of its output, Phoenicia had a 45 percent market share. Customers included Coca-Cola, Carlsberg, and Heineken. I felt that if we could recruit A players to Phoenicia, treat the employees with respect, strive to create a great place to work, and improve our service to customers, we would turn this company around. These were lessons I had learned during my business life, and I knew they could really made a difference.

Our due diligence confirmed the disaster we saw on that first visit, but we clearly believed there was real opportunity there. We talked to customers and found that they were anxious to have a high-quality glass supplier in Israel. We met with the union to begin a process of learning how we could work together. We purchased Phoenicia in December of 2004.

About six months later, we asked the mayor of Yerucham, the small town in which Phoenicia was located, to visit the plant and have coffee with us. Amram Mitzna, a former two-star general in the Israel Defense Force, had previously been mayor of the third-largest city in Israel, Haifa, with three hundred thousand people, and came out of semiretirement to become the appointed mayor of Yerucham, a town with ten thousand people. I said to Mayor Mitzna, "Look, I've got two interests in Israel. I have a relatively new business interest and a long-standing philanthropic interest, which began when I first visited Israel in 1967. Among the things that are personally important to me is that the State of Israel should be a well-regarded success. Now that we have an investment in Yerucham, it's important to us that the town be successful. We won't have a healthy company in a community that itself is not healthy."

When I told Mitzna that we might consider a grant to help Yerucham, he was surprised. He said, "I am out trying to raise money all the time. You are the first person to call and ask me to come visit you to tell me you want to give us money." The initial grant enabled Mayor Mitzna to upgrade the mathematics curriculum and create two computer centers for the city's public education system.

What followed at Phoenicia was textbook execution. Moshe Weksler, the CEO of Israel Equity Ltd., our private equity holding company, had recruited a number of A players, including a new Phoenicia CEO, Amnon Cohen. Seven of the company's eight top executives were new hires. We hired a number of engineers to improve and better maintain the equipment. We installed a full-time quality assurance staff. We listened to our employees. In conjunction with our union, we increased the wages of the employees and improved the working conditions in the plant.

Our first investments in equipment were new inspection machines to detect quality problems. Then we installed a new production line. Later, we hired two full-time gardeners and cleaned up the outside property, planting grass, bushes, and trees. We repaired toilets and showers, and painted and cleaned all restrooms. In addition, we added air conditioning to the offices and put in new computer systems.

As CEO Amnon, who has led much of the change, puts it:

Mort is always looking at the glass as half full, not half empty. Many of the new management employees are here because of him. He pushed us to bring more skillful people in, and it cost a lot of money. But he's looking at this long term. He cares about the people and the future. He's investing in management no matter what the result is on the books the next month or so. He'll say, "We need more engineers in the plant, or we need more help in human resources. Hire them."

Right now, we are sending workers to Germany for training at one of the world's most efficient glass plants. We started with sending top management, then the second level, and now the machine operators. There are twenty-five people in all going for training to this state-of-the-art facility in Germany. We started English lessons with Berlitz for people who go there. They visit Germany for two weeks at a time, and they learn better ways to work the machines. We are truly investing in people, something that had not been done at Phoenicia for many years. Employees are seeing the difference, and they appreciate it a lot.

Not surprisingly, the results are coming in. Quality is up. Plant utilization has increased. Factory accidents are down. Market share has been gained. Revenues continue to grow. The company has become nicely profitable. Our vision for Phoenicia is to make it a highly desired workplace in Yerucham and one of the greenest factories in the south of Israel. Already, it is the only company in Israel that recycles container glass—some forty thousand metric tons yearly.

Amram Mitzna, who recently left Yerucham after his highly successful five years as mayor, explains the situation:

> This has been one of the most neglected, underprivileged remote towns in all of Israel. You did not live in this city if you were looking for an easy place to live. It is a city of mostly immigrants from Morocco, Russia, and other places. Before Mort came here, Phoenicia Glass Works was a place that was going to be shut down. There was nothing there but lost hope and despair. Now the workers are proud. You can get much more from people when they feel they belong.

How do I have an influence over this and my other business interests in Israel when I live six thousand miles away? Once a month, I receive a set of financial reports from our chief financial officer. More important, I am on the telephone every Sunday morning with IEL CEO Moshe Weksler going over the latest issues on plant safety, product quality, customer satisfaction, revenue, and profit. Every Sunday, we're joined by either the CEO of Phoenicia or the CEO of Bikur Rofe, another company we own that operates a chain of health care clinics in Israel and employs about six hundred people, including 350 doctors.

We focus on three priorities: (1) making the companies great places to work, (2) fully satisfying our customers, and (3) fully satisfying our shareholders. Written minutes are taken of each of these telephone meetings so that nothing gets lost in memory or translation. Every Sunday our meeting starts with the reading of the previous session's minutes.

I now visit Israel three times a year. About four days of each trip are devoted to business; six or seven days are spent on our philanthropic activities. I'll have dinner each evening with senior staff, and I'll meet with management and tour each of our facilities during the day.

We did not get this right immediately. When we bought Phoenicia, we knew we were on a multiyear program to improve that plant. We didn't try to do it all at once. We replaced the chief executive whom we inherited, and then within six months we let his replacement go. The reason? The new CEO was content to just get by, and getting by was not good enough for us. We wanted to build something special.

We still have more work ahead of us. There are more investments that need to be made and more efficiencies to achieve. But we're making excellent progress. Recently, some Mandel Foundation board members visited Phoenicia and listened to the union stewards' take on what has happened. Here is what one of the union stewards said:

> Before Mandel, we felt we were working to survive. Now we feel we are working to build something. What's going on today compared to the problems of the past, we see it as a miracle. We have been moved by the change. People who have been working many years here are going to the synagogue blessing the Mandel family.

This success represents my whole belief system. In a relatively short period of time, we implemented every core principle: hire A players; create a great work environment; treat people with respect; execute well; serve your customers. We brought the employees up to a reasonable standard. We wanted our workers to have good jobs and be fairly paid. Today, they're proud to work at Phoenicia and fully appreciate their new environment.

We know that our investment will all come back. That's the lesson. Further, I am convinced that it is in our best interests to help strengthen the community in which our business is located. This isn't about Mort Mandel's social consciousness. It's purely enlightened self-interest. Phoenicia Glass Works is proof of that.

Now when I visit the plant, I see people who are fully engaged with what they're doing. The faces smile and always acknowledge my presence. It's not unusual for a worker to wrap his arms around me and give me a hug.

Now I know that, if I ever need it, I can go to Yerucham for a natural high.

CHAPTER 14

Yes, I Can!

DURING WORLD WAR II WHEN I WAS IN THE U.S. ARMY, I was once put in charge of transporting some fifteen wounded American soldiers from an army hospital in Memphis, Tennessee, to another hospital in the south. A few hours after we left Memphis by train, we stopped at a railway station in a town in the Deep South and were about to go into a Fred Harvey restaurant for lunch when a greeter stopped us at the door. He wouldn't permit the few African American soldiers in our group to enter this segregated restaurant. I saw that there was a long table of about ten German prisoners, dressed in fatigues with foot-high POW letters on their backs, eating inside. I objected violently to this ugly discrimination, but to no avail. In the end, I took all of our soldiers away, put aside our meal vouchers, and bought sandwiches from a nearby street vendor. We ate our lunch standing outside.

I hadn't realized it at the time, but it was probably the first true leadership decision I had ever made. In Officer Candidate School, I was taught the importance of command presence and the obligation to always satisfy the needs of your troops before you satisfy your own. Yet my decision at that Southern rail station came from a conviction deep inside me that what had occurred was unfair and unjust. I had to stand up against it. Any other decision would not have occurred to me. The incident brings to mind what leadership expert and consulting editor on this book, Warren Bennis, has long said: "Managers do things right. Leaders also do the right things."

Thousands of books have been written on leadership. Often they converge on some basic ingredients: vision, passion, and integrity, among others. What most of these books and lessons often miss is as crucial to leadership as intellectual brainpower and work ethic: The belief that each of us can make a positive and powerful difference on other people and on society. You need to believe in the power of one.

Too often, we're led to accept that the world's problems are too daunting to solve, that many business challenges are impossible to conquer. We throw our arms up in the air when we think not enough gets done in Washington. We give up on some of the deep social issues in the world because we feel they are insurmountable. Instead of thinking "Yes, I can," we're often taught, "No, I can't."

All your life, you are conditioned to think that being a success requires some kind of breakthrough. That is not what usually happens. Success is rare, we're told. It comes against overwhelming odds. It is a long and a hard struggle. Only a relatively few succeed. Fear can overpower you. If Steve Jobs or Bill Gates or Mahatma Gandhi believed that they were unlikely to achieve success, we probably would never have heard of them. If I believed it, I wouldn't be writing this book.

The truth is, you can aim to be anyone you want to be. Yes, you need the raw material to work with—the intellectual firepower and the values, passion, and work ethic to make something of yourself. But leadership starts by saying, "Yes, I can." Call it confidence or optimism or faith. Norman Vincent Peale famously called it "the power of positive thinking." Believing in the power of one is transforming. I profoundly believe that anyone can strive to be the next Abraham Lincoln or the next Warren Buffett, just as profoundly as I believe that someone can create the next Microsoft or Apple. But making something of yourself must begin with a moment of truth when you firmly believe that you are in control of your life and your fate.

Remember the children's story "The Little Engine That Could"? It is the tale of a stranded train unable to find an engine willing to take it over difficult terrain to its destination. Only a little blue engine is willing to accept the challenge. While repeating the mantra "I think I can, I think I can," the little engine overcomes what at first seems an impossible task. It is a story meant to awaken the sense of possibility in us, a sense that too often is stifled due to our personal circumstances or the environment in which we are raised.

It could have been the time you were asked, as a child, to read a literary passage aloud in front of your class. Perhaps you stumbled over the lines, were scolded by a teacher, and laughed at by a few of your classmates. You allowed the episode to stay with you, to hold you back. You need to let it go, to understand that your life should not have changed in any significant way because of a single experience.

Self-confidence is the key to "Yes, I can." Where does it come from? Many sources. For me, one time it arrived in the form of an inspiring English teacher, Laura V. Edwards, at Glenville High School in Cleveland, who convinced me that I could achieve almost anything I wanted. More specifically, she once encouraged me to write a one-act play with my friend Milton Metz and submit it to a local radio station. Much to my surprise, that station took our play and produced it, and when we performed it on a Saturday, Ms. Edwards was there to encourage us.

Throughout my life, my mother, my brothers, and my friends reinforced the confidence that came from that experience. There were little things that added up: being put into an advanced class in fourth grade because I could do the work, winning academic scholarships from both of the two colleges to which I had applied, scoring unusually high in a U.S. Army classification test. You get these reinforcements as you succeed, and they build on each other.

You have to know you are or can be an A player. But having the right stuff doesn't ensure that you'll realize the promise of leadership. Some never taste success because either they don't try or they just get lost. They're in the wrong place at the wrong time with the wrong people around them.

Through most of this book, I've explored the principles or skills of leadership—from the conviction that you need to surround yourself with A players to a steadfast devotion to high-quality execution. But to become a leader, you need to believe in the power of an individual to achieve success. From this belief comes the self-confidence, strength, and resilience to persist in the face of disappointments, setbacks, and even failures.

Ultimately, it is what we teach at the Mandel Leadership Institute in Jerusalem, which I mentioned briefly in Chapter Eleven. All the graduates of this two-year program leave the school knowing one thing for sure: that they can, if they desire, strive to improve the larger society as a leader in education or the social sector. They can impact the world for the better. We teach them the fundamentals of leadership and change management. We teach the importance of values and educational philosophy. But what we really do is turn out people who are equipped and motivated to change the world and who believe they can.

Their stories are inspiring and motivational to me and to the many people they touch and influence. Each is evidence of a single individual's ability to make a true difference in this world of ours.

Consider Chezie Sagiv. Now fifty-one, he had joined the Israel Air Force at the age of eighteen and took to the skies in his first mission a year later at nineteen. For more than thirty years, Chezie flew fighter jets in several wars, had a couple of close experiences with death, and ultimately became a pilot instructor at the Israeli Air Force Academy and a full colonel. But as he approached his forties, Chezie wanted to change his life, devoting himself to the education of young people in Israel.

I'll let Chezie tell the story.

> I realized that our country badly needs an educational system that creates leaders. I want to make change and create peace between our country and our neighbors. I want to make Israel the best place in the world. But we are in a war situation. I decided to choose education over the military because everything starts from education.

In other words, Chezie wanted to change for the better the world he knew. As a military leader, he certainly had the right stuff, but he spoke the language of the military, and he wanted to have an impact in an area of society with which he was far less familiar. Chezie turned down the chance to be commander of an Air Force base; instead he earned his master's in education and then entered our two-year leadership program.

As Chezie puts it:

> I had been in a place where everyone had to listen to me as an instructor and commander and then I was in a place, the Mandel Leadership Institute, where I was just one student out of many. It was important for me to leave out the ego of a fighter pilot and Air Force commander.

I learned how to listen to others, and that is a very important part of being a student and a human being. The second important point was that I was exposed to philosophy and the importance of values for the first time in my life. I came home so excited because I knew it would make me a better human being. I knew it would change my life.

For the past ten years, Chezie has made his personal imprint on children as a very successful high school principal. This past year, he established a new high school near Jerusalem with twelve hundred students and a staff of 160. His vision includes focusing less on grades and more on values. "I want to teach children how to become better citizens and better human beings," he says, "how to contribute to society and to their country."

Chezie is changing the world, one person at a time. We were lucky to find him, put him through a transformative experience, and cut him loose. Now he's out to build a better world. He has said to himself, "Yes, I can," and Chezie is getting others to believe it as well.

And then there is Dalia Peretz, a Mandel fellow whose revolutionary thinking has done what many considered impossible only a few years ago: she established a school for both Jewish and Arab children in Israel. As the coprincipal, Peretz has brought these children together to study side by side, learning each other's languages and cultures, from kindergarten to the twelfth grade. The simple yet profound idea: by coming together in a classroom, Arabs and Jews can understand that their common humanity is more important than any differences that divide them. The school teaches a strong set of values that includes respecting differences and promoting social and cultural equality.

In every class, there are two teachers: a Jew and an Arab. The students in each class are divided between Jews and Arabs. At many of the desks, they're paired up together, Jews and Arabs, boys and girls. The lessons are taught in Hebrew and Arabic. And the school has not one but two principals: Peretz, who is Jewish, and Ala Khatib, who is Arab.

Like all of us, Peretz is a product of her upbringing. She was born in a small development town in the south of Israel where most of the immigrants were from North Africa, including her parents. They spoke Arabic at home because her mother didn't know Hebrew. Her father studied the Torah and worked in a factory. Peretz grew up to become a high school teacher in Jerusalem. She came to our program in 1999 with the objective of accomplishing meaningful social change through education. She tells the story well:

My background is a complexity for someone who comes to a Jewish homeland where Arabs are a minority. This is the complexity I grew up with. By religion, we were Jewish. But we also had the Arab culture at home. It was a kind of dissonance in the early years of my life. I had to settle this complexity and see the advantages in it.

As a Mandel fellow, I wrote a multicultural curriculum that would enable kids from different cultures and religions to study together. It was a life-transforming experience. Another Mandel graduate, Lee Gordon, wrote the vision for the school. I took the principal position in the first year. The school was very small, with just dozens of kids in the beginning. It was something so new and radical that it was shocking for people. Many were shocked to hear that there could be a school where Jews and Arabs choose to study and grow up together. But the shock of it was part of changing public consciousness.

Although the school was very small in the beginning, now it is more than five hundred kids. We've discovered that it's possible to grow up together and still keep your identity, that you can conduct a better dialogue and relationship with others because you are more certain about who you are. It makes you a better human being. You are a richer person. You are more respectful to other people. I saw that it is very possible for Arabs and Jews to live together, each secure in their own traditions.

Thanks to Dalia Peretz's experimental school, there are now more of these innovative schools throughout Israel. And after a ten-year stint as coprincipal, she is now on to a new, important challenge: to finds ways to help students from lower socioeconomic backgrounds attain high educational achievement.

Finally, there is Ruth Lehavi, who came to the Mandel Leadership Institute in 1992 as the principal of an experimental high school and who had a dream of bringing together both secular and religious children in a single school. She began planning her new school in Jerusalem while still in the Mandel training program.

The school opened in September of 1995, two months before Yitzhak Rabin, the Israeli prime minister, was assassinated by a right-wing radical Orthodox Jew who was opposed to Rabin's signing of the Oslo Accords.

Lehavi remembers the shocking tragedy as if it were yesterday:

On the day of the Rabin assassination, we gathered all the children and talked to them about what happened. People were crying. Some of the parents said their only ray of hope was that their kids were in our school, which was aimed at teaching tolerance. The Rabin assassination made it clear that there was a critical need to bring together these two parts of Israeli life. There was great anxiety that we were building two different societies.

But not everyone liked the idea when we first proposed it. The religious department in the municipality wouldn't accept it. For them, it was taking religious kids out of a religious atmosphere and endangering them by mingling them with kids from secular families. They feared that the kids would stop being religious once exposed to another way of life. And it was unheard of that nonreligious teachers would be teaching Judaism.

To plan this project, I sat in the Mandel building with other educational professionals once a week for three or four hours. It was like realizing a dream. These were professional people who gave me the confidence that I could overcome all the obstacles and hurdles. When we first brought together a group of secular and religious kids, they began singing songs and talking. It worked, and I was amazed.

We started from kindergarten and grades 1 and 2. A year later, we went to grades 3 and 4. Our first graduates are now at the university level, and there are now ten thousand children in these kinds of schools throughout Israel.

The children are in the same class together. One teacher is religious, and the other is secular. There are few classes that are separated. We try to insure that the kids will hear both voices. Even if they are in a class with a religious teacher, they will hear from time to time from a nonreligious instructor. They are exposed to all thinking. We teach them to be more open minded and tolerant and to see the differences as both a challenge and an opportunity.

The stories of Chezie Sagiv, Dalia Peretz, and Ruth Lehavi are all unique—and all have in common the need to believe in yourself and in your ideas to make the world a better place. It starts with saying and believing "Yes, I can," just as I did in standing up to an intolerable injustice while in the U.S. Army so many years ago.

CHAPTER 15

Some Beacons to Steer By

THROUGHOUT THIS BOOK, I've tried to create a resource for people in search of ideas that can increase understanding and help them approach life in a more meaningful way. I didn't invent a lot of this, but I used these beliefs and ideas and still do. They work for me. If you like one, use it. It may work for you, too.

That's my attitude regarding all my other ideas as well. I present them in the hope that they will be useful to leaders and managers in all organizations. Underlying almost all of them is the central belief that a quality organization and a quality planning process can both improve results and help take some of the stress out of a busy life. Just as an example, a good place to start is where so many of us spend so much time: in meetings.

Running a Meeting

In the 1970s, Ralph Besse, then chairman of the Cleveland Electric Illuminating Co., invited me to join that company's board. It turned out to be a major learning experience for me. Trained as a lawyer, Ralph had gone to the Harvard Business School for its Advanced Management Program. He then put into practice what he learned at Harvard. More important, he ran the best formal meetings that I had ever attended.

Anyone who works in management spends a lot of time in meetings. Often people who run meetings show too little respect for the time of others. Their meetings can start late and end late. Too often people who lead meetings do not sufficiently prepare. Ralph was the very model of efficient organization. His meetings were carefully planned. Considerate of every person in the room, he ran a meeting by the clock.

I copied nearly everything Ralph did. He taught me that a well-run meeting begins before anyone shows up. All together, over time, here is what I learned:

- The agenda and any reports should be sent well in advance so that people arrive prepared to discuss the key issues.
- Seating should be carefully managed, never random. Every seating arrangement can be a potential learning opportunity, a chance for an experienced board member to teach a newcomer, or perhaps a chance to create a spark between two senior members.
- An agenda should be on the table at all places. No one should ever sit in a meeting wondering what will be discussed.
- Everyone should have a three-ring binder with every page consecutively numbered and with tabbed sections so that no one gets lost during a discussion.
- The person chairing the meeting should have a set amount of time set aside for every agenda item.
- The leader of the meeting should maintain a rolling assignment list so that the status of assigned tasks during any meeting can be followed up until completed.

- There should be a meeting schedule, usually for the next twelve months, so that members have advance knowledge of upcoming time commitments.

If I chair meetings, 90 percent of them will start on time, and all will end on time. This makes time—one of the most precious things a busy professional has—predictable. What that means is that when people have a meeting with you, they know they have to be on time and that you respect their time also.

Another useful ingredient on this list is humor. It helps to use a touch of humor to relax a group. I may poke fun at myself (never at anyone else) or at something that may come up. It can change the climate in the room.

Living a Stress-Free Life

How I run a meeting is, in many respects, how I run my life. Every workday is carefully planned. I ascribe much of my success to this process. I trace some of this to the high personal standards that my mother built into our consciousness and some to the management training I received in the military during World War II.

My routine is based on my commitment to maintaining my good health. This includes diet, exercise, and sufficient rest. I have a routine every morning. The first thing I do is physical fitness: thirty minutes of stretches and strengthening. Twice a week, a fitness trainer is with me for an hour. Then I plug in the coffee and drink a bottle of water. I eat a few tangerines and go into my office at home. At this point, the clock often tells me it's 4 AM.

A big part of my activity is organized in three-ring binders. In my home offices in Florida and New York, I have about forty of them, some being duplicates of binders in my business office in Cleveland. They detail the significant issues I'm dealing with in either business or philanthropy. I know where to put things and where to find things. That allows for quick retrieval of the facts I need to know in order to think through an issue and act on it.

Making the shift from an informal personal system to a formal one will yield better results. You'll have more control over your time and your responsibilities. A formal schedule can mean you sit down on a regular basis for important meetings, and you have things in writing.

My main point: I find that this operating style takes much of the stress out of my life.

The Value of Long-Term Relationships

All through my life, I've tried to build relationships with people who make things happen in my world. It's how I live my life. Leadership depends on relationships. I cultivate enduring relationships with people I admire and trust, from bankers and lawyers to my closest partners in business and philanthropy. We started with a law firm in 1958, and they still do some of our work. We started with a Cleveland bank in the late 1940s, and we're still with them. In 1955, I hired Phil Sims, who eventually became chief financial officer of Premier Industrial Corp. He still works with me as a consultant. My closest social friend, Leonard Ronis, and I met in the third grade, and we still see each other regularly.

Life is a collection of relationships. Building strong, lasting relationships should be as conscious a process as any other you manage. That's not to say that when you're disappointed, you fail to move on. As one example of this, we hired our public accounting firm in 1954, but we left fifty-one years later in 2005 and only after three years of frustration. Strong relationships take time and commitment. In our case, such relationships have been very positive.

In the philanthropic area, we sometimes commit to a long-term, ongoing and sustained funding effort where we stay the course until there is clear reason to feel we have done as much as we should. We do this because the most basic and significant challenges of human suffering and human accomplishment are persistent, deep, and constantly evolving. The idea is to develop a continuing relationship involving both parties in strategy and outcomes.

The Key to a Successful Family Partnership

Early on, my brothers and I agreed to two rules that could never be broken. First, we would not make a major decision unless all of us were in agreement. Any one of us always had veto power. Believe me, there were plenty of disagreements over the years. On all the major moves, any one of us could have killed it—and sometimes did. There were any number of 2-1 votes that inevitably led to disappointment. That early policy decision put our relationship ahead of any single business issue, and it has worked.

The second lesson was learned in the late 1940s when we hired Jack's son-in-law as a salesman. Within six months, we knew this was sending a negative message to our staff about growth opportunities for nonfamily members. That's when we agreed to create a no-nepotism rule in the company. With that decision, we committed to making our company a true meritocracy. We believed that we might not keep some A players in our organization if our key positions were filled by family members only.

No doubt, we "cheated" ourselves out of some talent as a result, but we saved ourselves a lot of potential difficulty. It meant that none of us would ever be lobbied, either by each other or by other family members, to hire or to promote a family member in our business. This became a nonissue, allowing us to run the company on the basis of individual performance and results achieved, not on who was related to whom. We know, of course, that other founders have acted differently and often with great success.

But in our case, ultimately our partnership endured because Jack, Joe, and I worked so well together. Many people who worked with us over the years saw the respect and admiration Jack, Joe, and I had for each other. Bob Warren, who had been president of Premier until he retired in 1990, had a front-row seat to the dynamics of our partnership. His insight into how it worked is instructive:

They were like the Three Musketeers. They always stood up for each other. They had an admiration for each other's strengths, and they used each other's strengths. Joe was a creative genius in marketing and in the field. Jack's strengths had to do with decision making and always bringing a calm and thoughtful approach to the business. And Mort was the leader and the builder; the structured, highly disciplined manager; the person who got things done.

You put those three things together, and the three of them made things happen. If one of them argued about something that the others didn't agree on, they worked it out. They never let small problems interfere with getting results because they agreed on the big things. They all shared the same objective: they wanted Premier to be a great company.

It was brotherly love that made it work.

Stretching People Beyond Their Comfort Zone

As a leader, you're responsible for the growth of your people. So it's important to give them the opportunity to step up and get involved in new things that challenge them. You can't wait until they are 100 percent ready. Instead, look for a time when they are, in your judgment, 70 to 80 percent ready for a new challenge. Basically, most people will find the capacity to stretch and meet the challenge.

Years ago, GE did a study of the people who made the fastest climb in that corporation. The majority of them said they had the good fortune at one time to work for a particular executive who had a profound impact on their career and who taught them basically what leadership was all about. This is why I so strongly believe that growing leaders requires them to be under a constant and continuous stretch, always aimed at personal growth.

When you provide guidance and help to subordinates, they have to know they can come to you when they're stuck. And they need to know it's okay to come back for help. Coaching skills are a quality I want all of our leaders to have—the ability to diagnose a person's strengths and weaknesses and push her to use her strengths to the maximum. Peter Drucker said it best: leadership is the alignment of strengths that make weaknesses almost irrelevant.

Think Big, Start Small

Make your mistakes when you're driving at twenty-five miles per hour, not when you're going sixty-five. Then, rev it up as you learn. The most important learning will occur when you start small and can freely experiment and gain experience. Starting small also overcomes the need to initially think big. It frees you to take some time to discover what "big" and "successful" could be. We started a number of new and eventually thriving businesses by giving one person an office and a simple initial business plan.

Through my years at Premier, in addition to twelve acquisitions, we created five new divisions from scratch. As an example, after spending a year in research on the possibility of adding welding alloys that were easier to use and longer lasting, we brought aboard a division leader to slowly develop a growth plan.

We didn't hire any other people on day one. We hired just a single motivated leader. It wasn't until many months later that we made our first sale. It took years to reach the desired level of two hundred sales reps throughout the United States. But the great benefit of starting small is that the mistakes you make in learning a new business do not hurt as much, and thus you can afford to make a lot of them. If you build too quickly, mistakes can be very expensive. Operating at a more modest level gives you the time you need to find the road to success.

It's the same in our philanthropic efforts. The Mandel Center for Leadership in the Negev, the southern part of Israel that tends to lag behind in progress and economic development, started out as a small idea and bloomed into a major initiative. The goal: to increase the number and the effectiveness of public leaders to help communities in the Negev. Varda Shiffer, who ran the Mandel Foundation in Israel until June 2012, tells the story:

We started in the Negev in August of 2004 with one full-time person, a car, and a telephone. We began speaking to people in the field about what was needed and what we could offer. After two months, we had requests for a leadership program. There was an important need, and yet no one was there to teach leadership skills. For seven or eight months, two of us worked on developing a leadership program. We borrowed faculty from our Mandel Leadership Institute. Soon, we had three leadership programs going. We were working day and night. We took temporary premises in Beer Sheva for a year, and at the end of our second year we established a very functional training center. Now, we have ten staff people and seven programs. As always we started small, and now have grown to where we are having a real impact on the quality and performance of leaders in public sector jobs.

One of our main objectives is to convince people that it is in their power to improve their own lives. Communities can increase their chances of improving their life if they have a plan and learn from their experience.

90 Percent Budgeting

This is a simple exercise that can lead to a lot of creative thinking. Every year, I ask my team to do the equivalent of reducing their budgets by 10 percent. Then I ask them what they would do with that newly freed 10 percent—and they must consider those projects on hold along with those that had been temporarily removed from the budget. Why? I want them to prioritize the resources they have and think about how that money and time can be spent most thoughtfully. The exercise leads to fascinating discussions and often enables us to rethink how we deploy our staff and dollars.

Do It Better for Less

In every organization, there are many opportunities to do things better—for less. You need to be on the constant lookout for those opportunities. The nickels and dimes add up, every day, every week, every month.

Budgets are not entitlements. Conditions change. Expenses that were needed last year may not be needed this year. So there are new opportunities to make a difference.

At Premier, over many years, we built profit consciousness to the point where we had a 5 percent profit improvement goal in almost every department. About 5 percent of a group's expenses were to be cut every year. This saved literally millions for the company, and those millions dropped right to the bottom line. Many departments did not achieve their full goal, but always some did. This enabled us to accumulate major savings, often by reducing the costs of things like freight and travel or by simply lowering a standard that had been set too high.

When a department accomplished this goal, it was publicly celebrated. The department name was put on a plaque on the wall. Their successes were transparent to everyone. In that way, we deeply built the idea of doing better for less into the culture of Premier.

• • •

All these principles are part of who I am and how I live and work. I've dedicated my life to achieving the best possible result in everything I do, whether it's being a good employer, keeping a customer happy, combating human misery, or being a successful son, husband, and father.

Life for me has been a wonderful journey.

We make our own history in this world. We measure happiness and unhappiness, success and failure, by our own expectations and standards. I have never felt that I have "arrived." I know that the really important goals in life are never fully achieved. Reaching for these goals is the journey.

CHAPTER 16

If I Could Do It Over Again . . .

AS I APPROACH THE LATER YEARS OF MY LIFE, I've allowed myself to become somewhat more introspective. My hope is that by reading this book, you've discovered a man who fell in love with his world and the opportunities he saw everywhere. Some may think that I have worked exceptionally hard all my life. Truth is, I never considered it work and still don't. My dreams for achieving worthy goals have made every day a privilege. Mostly, I've lived a wonderful life because of all the exceptional people I've been lucky to know and learn from and work with. This is true, even more, for my personal life.

I have had a wonderful marriage. I was extraordinarily fortunate to fall in love with a woman, Barbara, who would be my wife and confidant for sixty-two years, and to have three loving children, Amy, Thomas, and Stacy; seven beautiful grandchildren; and now one great-grandchild.

I can close my eyes today and still hear my mother's voice, still feel her deep influence. Her values became my values. Her strength and her compassion became my own as well. For our family, she created a home, a refuge for us where we were safe, loved, respected, and encouraged to be the best we could be. I was blessed and lucky to have two brothers, Jack and Joe, who became very close friends and business partners. Our decision to go into business together in 1940 had profound consequences. We pursued a single dream, bringing all of our energy and focus to it.

Throughout my life, I've had the great benefit of learning from many teachers and mentors, from Laura V. Edwards, my English teacher at Glenville High School, who gave me the confidence that comes from being told you are smart and can do anything you want with your life, to the wisest management guru I ever met, Peter Drucker, who taught me that nothing matters more than surrounding yourself with exceptional people.

Indeed, I owe a huge personal debt to the many colleagues and associates who early on shaped my ideas and me: Henry Zucker, Herman Eigen, Stan Horowitz, Steve Hoffman, and Seymour Fox in the philanthropic world; John Colman, Bob Warren, Bill Hamilton, Phil Sims, and Stu Neidus in business.

I've come to believe that all of this—my entire effort in both the for-profit and nonprofit parts of my life—has been a search for fulfillment. For most of my life, I thought that the top of the mountain was success. In business, it was building companies, creating meaningful jobs for people, satisfying customers, being true to who you are. In philanthropy, success was investing in people with the vision, passion, and abilities to change the world. The journey I had been on was a journey to feel I had done something significant with my life, that I had become somebody.

Only recently I came to understand more clearly what true fulfillment means. It is not the size of your bank account or your stock portfolio. It's not whether you have a big house or a yacht or a private plane. And it's certainly not about getting your name in the paper.

It's about respecting yourself for who you are and how you have lived your life. Happiness for me is meeting my own expectations and those of the people I care about and love. Everything of virtue springs from the dedication, passion, even love, you bring to what you do. If there is a secret to a life well lived, it's simply to live a worthy and contributive life, striving to meet your expectations and the expectations of those you love and respect. It's why my regrets are few and far between.

It's a point I often try to reinforce when I meet young people who are initially interested in how I became a billionaire and later discover that there are more important lessons here than making money. For many years, I have gone to the classes of Professor Richard Osborne at Case Western University's Weatherhead School of Management to speak with MBA students. Professor Osborne describes a recent visit this way:

> The class is a second-year elective called the Chief Executive Officer. We study CEOs during that class, and we're searching for best practices. We'll have a number of chief executives come into the course, including CEOs from American Greetings, Progressive, and other companies. Then there is Mort, who I tee up as "the billion-dollar man." That immediately gets their attention. None of them have ever met a billionaire before, and while they know how many numbers make a billion, they don't know what a billion dollars is. I explain that it's one thousand million. I tell them that if you had a billion and put the money in a passbook account with 5 percent interest, one day's return would be $137,000.
>
> Now, they're very interested in this guy Mort. How much money he has made loses its appeal quickly when they hear Mort speak about the absolute necessity of getting the very best people on your team, how to treat your customers exceptionally well, why execution is essential to success, and how values and integrity underlie everything he does. Mort has a way of making things deceptively simple, and his capacity to inspire is a huge part of who he is.

At the end of the first class, the students give him a standing ovation. It's completely spontaneous. They're electrified by what they've learned. But when he comes back for the second class, they give him a standing O when he comes in. I've never seen anyone greeted that way in my classes. The fact that he is a billionaire is no longer important to them. The ovation is about who he is and not what he made.

What would I do if I could do it over again? I would focus even more attention on finding, recruiting, and cultivating the A players on my team and on creating a great place for them to work. Early on, I settled too often. I kept too many B players in leadership roles when I could have had people with greater intellectual firepower and ability. In an economy powered by ideas, A players make all the difference in the world.

To my mind, the cost of settling was far greater than unrealized profit or opportunity. The cost was also in not having the kind of leadership throughout the organization that enriches the lives of other employees, and in not innovating more products and services that would benefit our customers. That is the price of settling. That is the cost you pay when you keep a B when you should have an A in a key leadership position. I was not as intense early on as I am today about the need to focus totally on getting A's in all of the important jobs.

Today, Israel Equity Ltd. and Bikur Rofe, both in Tel Aviv; Phoenicia Glass Works in Yerucham; Parkwood Corp. in Cleveland; and Parkwood Trust Co. in Wilmington are all great places to work. So are the several Mandel Foundation units in Israel. In many respects, but not to the same extent, so was Premier Industrial Corp. Only in my later years was I aware of the power of very deliberately building a great place to work.

Our great place to work puts family first. Our culture understands that it's important to allow someone to occasionally leave work during the day to see, for example, a child in a school play. When people make the decision to give themselves to an organization, a "family first" policy makes a difference. Plain and simple, this is a matter of self-interest. Treating people with respect, kindness, and consideration builds profits in the long run. A culture that encourages and respects family responsibilities forges a bond between employees and the organization that can bring deep mutual benefit.

One thing I fail to understand is why making a major commitment to A's is so hard to comprehend. Anyone who has ever had a direct report who was clearly an A has experienced the benefit of superior performance. Why do so many then settle for less? If we had 50 A players among the top 150 senior managers at Premier, perhaps we could have had 100. If I had known what I know today, I would have moved heaven and earth to get those 100 A players. I would have seen that as our greatest opportunity. For more than thirty years, I ran a public company that was making so much money, we could have easily afforded to invest in more A's.

It just took even more conviction than I had. A perfect example was a division of ours that was the best-performing company in its competitive set. Its products were of very high quality. Its customers were more than satisfied with the level of service provided. It was a solid, steady cash producer with high margins day in and day out, and it was run by a series of B players who were largely excellent maintenance managers but not transformative leaders. Although there was consistent innovation in the product line that the company sold, more imagination and creative thinking could have turned this division into a major growth vehicle for us. Instead, it was just a steady cash cow.

I believe that almost any company can be a growth business if you have the right people in the right jobs. I'd stake my reputation on it. If you have an A team and seek to satisfy customers and employees both, you can make almost any business a growth business. That is totally true for the social sector as well.

I'm often asked why I still work hard, why my calendar is filled with activity—one-on-one meetings, committee and board sessions, and travel to New York, Cleveland, London, Tel Aviv, and Jerusalem. The answer is easy: I love what I do. Human capital and financial capital together are an awesome combination. That capital can be used to touch souls and change lives. It can attract first-class leadership to any organization, and thereby improve higher education, fuel neighborhood urban renewal, offer inspiration and purpose to education, and secure a successful future for institutions and those who benefit from them. My goal is to use the human and financial capital at our disposal to change the world.

I do not intend to retire. There are so many exciting and wonderful things to do, so many more candles to light, so much more journey in my search for meaning. The torch is in my hand, and I intend to hold it as high as I can—for as long as I can.

APPENDIX

[NAME] FACTBOOK INDEX

1. MASTER SCHEDULE CONTROL

2. CALENDAR OF EVENTS

3. MINUTES & ASSIGNMENTS

4. DISCUSSION ISSUE

5. DISCUSSION ISSUE

PARKWOOD CORPORATION

JJ/MLM Factbook

Master Schedule Control

Prepared By: JJ

Date Prepared: 9/22/2011

JJ Factbook		2012											2013
	JAN	FEB	MAR	APR	MAY	JUN	JUL	AUG	SEP	OCT	NOV	DEC	JAN
	7	17	30	21	19	16	14	17	15	5	12	1	5
	7:30 AM	3:30 PM	1:30 PM	11:30 AM	9:30 AM	3:30 PM	7:30 AM	3:30 PM	9:30 AM	7:30 AM	3:30 PM	11:30 AM	9:30 AM

PARKWOOD CORPORATION

Investment Committee
Calendar of Events

PREPARED BY: JJ
Prepared: 3/23/12

STANDARD ELEMENTS	JAN	FEB	MAR	APR	MAY	JUN	JUL	AUG	SEP	OCT	NOV	DEC
Review of Standard Legal Terms		X										
Risk Manager Review										X		
Review Asset Class Target Allocations			X						X			
Review Liquidity Target Allocation					X							
Review of Policies and Procedures:												
1.3 Confidentiality of Client Information	X											
2.1 Tier Definition Guidelines		X										
2.2 Concentration Guidelines			X									
2.3 What GP's Want in an LP Relationship				X								
2.4 Asset Manager Selection					X							
2.6 Miscellaneous Investment Principles						X						
2.7 Expectations of Parkwood Asset Managers												X
2.8 Manager Warning Signals											X	
2.12 Corporate Investment Policy Statement							X					
2.13 Taxable Client Investment Policy Statement								X				
2.15 Risk Management Policy									X			

PARKWOOD CORPORATION
JJ/MLM Factbook Meeting
April 20, 2012   3:30 PM

MINUTES: John Jones Factbook

DATE OF MEETING: March 30, 2012

DATE MINUTES ISSUED: March 31, 2012

PRESENT: Mort Mandel, John Jones

I. Organization
   A. We discussed the difficulty in finding the right candidate for the Investment Operations Analyst position. Though several candidates have been interviewed, no one has been identified for whom we would give an "enthusiastic yes." Therefore, we will continue to wait until we find the right candidate.

II. Team Building
   A. We discussed the development of the Investment Operations Department. For us to grow, it is necessary for us to continue to push down responsibility to others within the department to free up capacity for the department head and to give opportunities for growth to others in the department. We will continue to look for responsibilities that can be delegated within the department.

III. Internal Audit
   A. We discussed the review of audited financial statements received from our asset managers. JJ indicated that the review of the audited financial statements is one of the most effective tools we have in performing our operations reviews. Though we cannot rely solely on the work performed by the auditors, they have access to the financial records of our asset managers and are therefore in the best position to highlight if there are any issues with which we should be concerned. Therefore, it is important that we continue to be thorough in our review of the audited financial statements.

IV. Risk Management
   A. MLM indicated that he is pleased with the progress in developing the Investment Operations Review process. MLM suggested that JJ and WD continue to evaluate the operations review process and challenge whether all of the steps are necessary. He suggested scheduling a time to reevaluate the process and ensure that we are receiving the benefit from the amount of work done. This should be done on a regular basis with all complex processes.
   B. We discussed the need to develop a broad policy statement of how we will keep risk management visible. This should include concentration limits, geographic limits, and risk profile limits (by total portfolio and by asset class).

Assign This can be in a monthly or annual report and should be reviewed with the Investment Strategy Committee at least two times a year. JJ will work with Allan in drafting this document.

V. Process

A. The Due Diligence Sub-Committee recently discussed potential changes to the format of investment recommendations and investment reviews. The goal is to make the recommendations and reviews more consistent and to ensure that all important areas are covered. MLM agreed with the changes suggested by the Committee, noting that the analysts should continue to focus on evaluating the "who" within the organization.

B. We discussed the recent changes to the tier definitions and concentration guidelines. The purpose of the tier definitions is to segregate our managers into groups based on our evaluation of, and relationship with, a manager. The concentration guidelines allow us to manage risk by limiting the investment in an asset manager based on their tier and risk assessment. We discussed MLM's suggested changes that will be incorporated in the next draft of the policy. Assign

VI. Reports

A. We discussed a new project that was added to JJ's project list to work with Michael Rogers to modify the calculation of returns for large external cash flows. It is important to ensure that our reports comply with the Global Investment Performance Standards, particularly when we are presenting returns to clients in their annual reports.

VII. Department Development

A. MLM noted that while the Finance and Legal Process Sub-Committees have been effective in developing policies and procedures for these departments, the focus has primarily been on "management" with very little discussion on "leadership." We need to ensure that we are capturing a discussion on the philosophy and beliefs of the founders. It is only by documenting this philosophy that it can be handed on to members of the department. MLM suggested that JJ meet with the heads of each department to brainstorm potential topics to be included in the manual. This can include confidentiality, integrity, etc. Assign

VIII. Next Meeting

April 20, 2012 3:30 PM

PARKWOOD CORPORATION

Assignments
Pk115 (9-13-01)

Function:	JOHN JONES FACTBOOK MEETING				
Subject/Objective: JOHN JONES ASSIGNMENTS					
Originator:	JOHN JONES		DATE:	3/30/12	
No.	Description	Priority	Assigned to Initials	Date Assigned Started	Due Date
1	Make suggested changes to the tier definitions and concentration guidelines policies	1	JJ	3/30/12	4/6/12
2	Develop a broad policy statement on risk management for the Investment Department	1	JJ	3/30/12	4/20/12
3	Work with Joe Roman to make a change to update the Total Parkwood Marketable Investments report to reflect MLM's changes	1	JJ	2/17/12	4/20/12
4	Meet with the heads of the Legal and Finance Departments to brainstorm potential "philosophy" topics to be included in the manual	2	JJ	3/30/12	6/30/12
5	Review the Investment Operations department responsibilities	2	JJ	2/17/12	7/31/12
6	Perform a full review of the Investment Manual to identify outdated policies that can be eliminated	3	JJ	1/7/12	TBD
7	Identify additional courses of study to provide professional development	3	JJ	12/4/11	TBD

"DISCUSSION DRAFT"
STAFF DEVELOPMENT PLAN

DATE PREPARED: 04/19/12
PREPARED BY: JJ

STAFF MEMBER:	Jim Smith	START DATE: 4/18/08

CURRENT POSITION: Investment Operations Analyst
EFFECTIVE DATE: 4/18/12

DEPARTMENT: Investment Operations

OBJECTIVES:
1. Process all investment transactions.

2. Prepare and review monthly investment reports.

3. Provide support to the Secretary function of investment committees.

4. Review investment management fees.

ACTIONS:
1. Continue to delegate to Jim any questions or requests from other departments that need to be pursued.

2. Train Jim on drafting policies and procedures.

DUTIES TO DOWNLOAD:
1. Tansfer responsibility for processing investment transactions to Marie Stone.

RESULTS:
Jim has a solid grasp on the process for handling investment transactions. Over the next six months, I would like to see Jim train Marie Stone on this responsibility to free up additional capacity.
As we do so, this will allow me to train Jim on the drafting of policies and procedures and continue to increase his responsibility in responding to questions and requests by other departments. He is easily coached and eager to learn.

NEXT POSITION: Manager of Investment Operations
TARGET DATE: 4/18/13

PARKWOOD CORPORATION
Investment Committee
May 17, 2012

	Assigned	Tab/Sched
I. Review of Minutes and Assignments	John Smith	3.0
II. Primer on Hedge Fund Beta	Jane Smith	4.0
III. Monthly Asset Class Reviews	Analysts	5.0
IV. General Commentary		
a. Risk of Leverage Aversion	Jane Smith	6.1
b. In-House Management	Robert Jones	6.2
c. Behavioral Finance	Harry Dewey	6.3
V. Market Update	Lee White	7.0
VI. Recent Government Initiatives Impacting Investment Managers	Mark Black	8.0
VII. Investment Policies and Procedures		
a. 2.4 Asset Manager Selection	John Smith	9.0
VIII. Update to Policy and Procedures Manual	John Smith	
IX. Next Meeting June 14, 2012 9:00 AM		

ACKNOWLEDGMENTS

IT HAS BEEN SAID THAT A FRIEND IS THE MOST GENEROUS GIFT YOU CAN GIVE YOURSELF. In that sense, I've been extremely generous.

Because this book is less biography and more a book of the ideas that I believe led to my success, I've not been able to mention or thank many people who have played important roles in my life. They all have the intellectual firepower, the values, the passion, and the work ethic that has made me better for knowing them.

Each of them has shared different parts of my journey, and I thank them for their friendship, their wise counsel, their loyalty, and their love.

First and foremost, I thank my wife, **Barbara Mandel**, for so thoroughly sharing my life with me. I can't imagine having lived this life without her by my side—and she has been there for sixty-two years. When I attend a charitable event at which Barbara has a leading role, I'm especially proud to be introduced as her spouse. We have been blessed with three wonderful children, **Amy**, **Thom**, and **Stacy**, and seven grandchildren, Alicia, Daniela, Willie, Jack, Lili, Olivia, and Daniel. And now I have one great-granddaughter, Amora.

In this book I've often mentioned my brothers, **Jack** and **Joe**. For most of my life, they were my two best friends, my partners in business and philanthropy, my teachers, and my pals, through thick and thin. They made my journey through life all the richer.

Leonard Ronis, whom I have known since the third grade, and **Milton Metz**, who has been a close friend since high school, shared my wonderful experience at Glenville High School, and I still count them as good friends today.

Premier was a success because of the team we were able to assemble and keep together over many years. That team included **Bob Warren**, **Bill Hamilton**, **Phil Sims**, **Bruce Johnson**, **Terry Taylor**, **Diedra Gold**, and **John Colman**, among many other key players.

Bob Warren, who rose to become president of Premier and was an exceptional, gifted leader, contributed to many of the key ideas that led to my firm beliefs, particularly the value of disciplined planning and superior execution.

Bill Hamilton, who succeeded Bob as president, was a superior operating executive.

Phil Sims, as Premier's chief financial officer and later vice chairman, provided much thoughtful insight over many, many years.

John Colman was the investment banker who helped take Premier Industrial Corp. public in 1960, served on our board from 1958 until our merger in 1996, and has been a business and philanthropic adviser and friend ever since.

Tony Pishkula, **Brad Smith**, **Jon McCloskey**, **Jim Fox**, and **Mark Madeja** make up the senior team of Parkwood Corp. This group of exceptional talent has helped make our private trust company a world-class performer. **Stu Neidus**, who was an executive vice president at Premier, remains a trusted business adviser on whose judgment I rely heavily.

Sally Wertheim, **Henry Goodman**, **Morris Offit**, and **Stephen Hoffman** have been longtime advisers and friends, as well as Mandel Foundation board members. Their advice and friendship over the years has enriched my life, and they are today still among my most trusted foundation associates.

Annette Hochstein took over as president of the foundation after the death of my close colleague Seymour Fox in 2005. Annette did a spectacular job of leading and growing the Mandel Leadership Institute and our many philanthropic activities in Israel. In July of 2010, **Varda Shiffer** succeeded Annette as president of Mandel Foundation-Israel. Varda designed and developed the Mandel Center for Leadership in the Negev and was that center's first director.

Our brilliant staff of educators and leaders has made the Mandel Foundation in Israel one of the brightest candles I have lit in my life. Other senior leaders, **Pierre Kletz**, **Eli Gottlieb**, and **Mordecai Nisan**, have accomplished small miracles.

I have studied the richness and wisdom of our Jewish tradition for many years now with a brilliant, charismatic, and courageous member of the rabbinical community in Jerusalem. **Rabbi David Hartman** is the founder and leader of the Shalom Hartman Institute, a scholarly center for those who aspire to gain a deep understanding of our Jewish tradition. My sessions with Rabbi Hartman over a thirty-year period have helped me better understand the profound impact Judaism has had on shaping the values and beliefs of Western civilization.

Moshe Wexler is my business partner and the CEO of Israel Equity Ltd. (IEL), our private equity firm in Israel. Moshe brings deep experience and great wisdom to our business operations there. **Dov Tadmor**, with whom I started IEL, is a close personal friend and adviser.

Many volunteers and professionals have shaped my work in the social sector. These include **Arthur Naperstek, Phil Bernstein, Sanford Solender, Herbert Millman, Arthur Rotman, Alan Finkelstein, Herman Eigen, Stanley Horowitz, Herman Stein, Michael Benz, Esther Leah Ritz, Lee Shulman, Charles Ratner, Morris Offit, Sanford (Buddy) Silberman**, and **Michael White**.

Donna Cuilli, my trusted and very loyal executive assistant in Cleveland, helps me every working day, no matter where I am—in Florida, New York, or Jerusalem.

JoAnn White is my right and often left hand in helping me run the Mandel Foundation on a day-to-day basis.

Over the years, I have been extremely fortunate to work with and alongside many world-class educators and to call them my friends. They include **Scott Cowen**, a former board member of Premier who is now president of Tulane University; **Menachem Ben-Sasson**, the president of Hebrew University in Jerusalem; **David Ellenson**, president of Hebrew Union College; **Menachem Magador** and **Hanoch Guttfreund**, former presidents of Hebrew University; and **Rivka Carmi**, president of Ben Gurion University. I'm proud to note that another prominent educator, **Jehuda Reinharz**, the former president of Brandeis University, is now the president of the Mandel Foundation. Other important Israeli colleagues include **MP Avishay Braverman**; **Yehuda Raveh**, my principal Israeli legal adviser; retired ambassador **Moshe Arad**; **Alan Hoffmann**; **Moshe Vigdor**; **Shlomo Mor-Yosef**; and **James Snyder**.

I also thank **Richard Osborne**, a professor of management at the Weatherhead School at Case Western University, who also serves as a director of Parkwood Corp. and is the educator with whom I have had the longest continuing relationship. Richard has been a trusted friend and mentor for almost a quarter of a century.

And finally, I acknowledge the team that helped me write this book: my collaborator, John A. Byrne; my wife, Barbara; and a number of dedicated readers, largely friends and colleagues, including Annette Hochstein and **Dan Pekarsky**, a former professor of philosophy at the University of Wisconsin and now a senior consultant to the Mandel Foundation.

They read the manuscript meticulously with their usual wisdom, common sense, and curiosity, and made copious comments through many drafts. This book is better because of their attention to detail.

THE AUTHORS

Morton L. Mandel is a leading philanthropist, business leader, and social entrepreneur. With his two brothers in 1940, he helped create Premier Industrial Corp., one of the more successful companies in the history of the New York Stock Exchange. As chairman and CEO of Premier from 1957 until 1996, Mandel brought the company public in 1960. He then led Premier to record profit and revenue for thirty-four out of the next thirty-six years.

Mandel now serves as chairman and CEO of Parkwood Corp. and its wholly owned subsidiary Parkwood Trust Co. He also serves as chairman and CEO of the Jack, Joseph, and Morton Mandel Foundation.

John A. Byrne, the former executive editor of *BusinessWeek* and editor in chief of *Fast Company* magazine, is the author or coauthor of ten other business books, including two *New York Times* best sellers. With legendary General Electric Co. CEO Jack Welch, he wrote *Jack: Straight from the Gut,* one of the most successful business books in history.

Index